STORIES FROM THE TAILOR

Stories from the Tailor

Edited and Translated by
Aindrias Ó Muimhneacháin

THE MERCIER PRESS
CORK and DUBLIN

The Mercier Press Limited
4 Bridge Street, Cork
24 Lower Abbey Street, Dublin 1

ISBN 0-85342-884-0

Stories from the Tailor was originally published in Irish in 1978 under the title *Seanchas an Táilliúra*.

Printed by Litho Press Co., Midleton, Co. Cork.

Contents

Introduction

The primary purpose of this translation of *Seanchas an Táil-liúra*[1] is to make its contents accessible to those in Ireland, and abroad, who might have been unable to fully or satisfactorily comprehend the original text in Irish which I edited for publication. All that material is included herein and in its original published sequence.

That miscellany was acquired from Tailor Timothy Buckley in his own house in Gearnapeaka, near Gougane Barra, Co. Cork, by Seán Ó Cróinín, a fulltime folklore collector employed by the Irish Folklore Commission, on an Ediphone recorder and transcribed verbatim by him between 14 July and 27 October 1942. His completed transcriptions are preserved in the archives of the Department of Irish Folklore, University College, Dublin. To the Head of that Department, Professor Bo Almqvist, I am indebted for having graciously permitted me to retranscribe, and edit for publication, that entire collection and for later having urged me to undertake its translation for the benefit of folklorists and others not versed in the Irish language.

The Tailor was a remarkable folk raconteur with an unconventional narrative flair. By way of introduction, for example, he might initially treat his audience to some jesting witticism, or to what would seem to be an inconsequential triviality, but from which he would proceed to some substantial yarn or traditional tale, or to tell of things wondrous or adventurous – all subtly related to his introductory levity. He might, too, deftly interpolate, between tales or anecdotes, a proverb or speech expression prompted by what he had just related, but he never would be put off his track – proving the excellence of his narratory craft. (This narrative process might not be apparent to readers of this volume nor of its original in Irish, for when editing the material, while ensuring that everything recorded was included, I did not always adhere to the order in which the Tailor had given what he had to tell but rather, for the convenience of general readers and students, I assigned the various inter-related items to homogeneous chapter sections.)

The Tailor too, in congenial company, was a great conversationalist. On everything he would have his own particular comprehension or solution, often quite out of the top of his head, but displaying an intelligence and an imagination which enabled him to unravel everything, rightly or wrongly, to his own satisfaction. His facility in that regard was really extraordinary, especially for one who, as he himself has informed us, was nearing nine years of age before he ever went to school and was only thirteen when apprenticed to tailoring.

Good though he was as a storyteller and conversationalist he knew hardly any of the great romantic or valour tales, though he held in the highest regard those who had these. This deficiency in his repertoire, I would suggest, was due to his having left home long before reaching manhood, and henceforth, and until he settled down in Gearnapeaka, his extensive travels took him to places where these tales were not being told nor was the Irish language being spoken. Of these places and of those with whom he became acquainted he had, however, much to tell.

His prime interest was in people – their kinship affinities, their traits and their peculiarities, and that is apparent from what we have got in this volume. Worthy of note in this regard is the precise and detailed manner in which he has traced his own ancestral lineage and that of the Sweeneys, the Twomeys and of other septs and individuals – where they had originally come from, where they settled, and who each of them, and their blood and marriage relations, married. He was extraordinarily well informed in that field, to the minutest detail.

Also he knew but comparatively few of the traditional songs in Irish, even though he had a good singing voice. His song repertoire seemed to have been limited mainly to jocular English ditties which, apparently, he had picked up on his travels.

It must have been on his travels too that he acquired the good mastery of English which he had. Still his facility in English was in no way comparable to the fluidity and the elegance of his Irish, the language of his youth. He also held in very high regard those others who had an eloquent command of that language. Note, for example, the high praise he has had for the inhabitants of Knockaunavona, 'All of them,' he has said, 'had wonderful Irish and great sayings. I often spent a night listening to some of them talking. All the Knockaunavona people had an extraordinary gift of speech. . . Speechwise those around Knockaunavona had no equals.'

Knockaunavona is a large townland in the parish of Kilgarvan,

Co. Kerry, and it was in Lounihan, an adjacent townland in the same parish, the Tailor was born on St Stephen's Day, 1863. There his father had acquired a sixty-acre farm, having been previously a dairyman[2] elsewhere in the same parish. Additional to the farm he had, conjointly with three others, grazing rights for sheep and cattle to a further 300 acres of mountain common-age. He had thirteen children – eleven sons and two daughters. The Tailor was the seventh son. The daughters and four of the sons emigrated to America, and another of the sons went to Australia. That was the fate of ever so many in those days. As the Tailor himself has related: 'It was only the best – all the young strong men – who went off. Had I had the use of my leg, I too would probably have gone. . . Anyone with any sort of infirmity had to stay here.'

An infirmity the Tailor had. When he was nine years old he was stricken by infantile paralysis, which left his right leg completely paralysed from the knee down. Its shank and foot grew no more, and ever afterwards he was dependent on a wooden crutch and stick.

Never did he in any way complain about his incapacity, other than his expression of regret at his having been deemed unacceptable for emigration to America. Notwithstanding, as a young man he roamed as far as Cork city and Dublin, and even to Scotland, plying his trade and with a view to seeing these places and to meeting and observing strange people.

In his latter years when due to old age he could no longer travel very far he remained confined to his own house in Gearnapeaka and its immediate environs.

There many visitors would come to him to be entertained by his discourses. One of these was Frank O'Connor, the distinguished writer, who has described him as being 'a small, crippled man with a round, merry face',[3] but had he got to know him earlier he would have found him to have been over six feet tall, even when he stood erect with the aid of his crutch.

It was in his latter days too that Seán Ó Cróinín came to him to record from him what he could of his store of traditional lore.

Previously he had not got to know him personally, but he knew of him by repute. Three months and two weeks, as we have said, he spent with him, but taking days off to write out what he had recorded from him on the ediphone – transcribing everything exactly as it had been said in every detail.

What Ó Cróinín thus procured from him is really only part of what he might have got had he been able to stay longer with him or had they got together some years earlier while the Tailor was still in his prime as a folk anecdotist. Regrettably, at the bidding of his employers, he had to move off elsewhere long before he had fully acquired for posterity what the Tailor had still to offer.

With him Seán Ó Cróinín had only barely taken time by the forelock. Three years later, in 1945 and at the age of eighty-two the Tailor was called to his eternal reward. As had been pre-arranged by himself, he was buried in the little graveyard overlooking the lake in Gougane Barra, and over his grave was erected a graceful headstone, designed and executed by his old friend, Séamus Murphy the eminent Cork sculptor.

AINDRIAS Ó MUIMHNEACHÁIN

1. Myself and My Kinsfolk

My grandfather was born in Coolavohir, Ballyvourney. His name was John Buckley. There were, at that time, two John Buckleys in Coolavohir, married to two sisters surnamed Lehane, daughters of Peter Larry.

Peter Larry had two gneeves of land. That land, I think, was in Moornaghbeg, Direenawling and Derrynasagart (in the parish of Ballyvourney). He had a son known as Peter Óg. He came to live in Gorteenflugh (above Ballingeary). There he had a farm and was married to a woman from Ballyvourney. One Sunday morning his wife's brothers came to Gorteenflugh and beat him up, and he survived only a year after that. What they had against him was that he had failed to go to Ballyvourney on a Whit Sunday to faction-fight.

The two John Buckleys were probably in some way related, but I don't know what the relationship was. The third of the Lehane sisters married Diarmaid 'ac Séamus Ó Conchúir, the poet. He lived in Derryraigue (in the parish of Glenflesk in Kerry).

Diarmaid was not too tall, but both of the John Buckleys who lived in Coolavohir, married to Peter Larry's other two daughters, were tall men. Someone, anyhow, remarked to Diarmaid 'ac Séamus: 'The two John Buckleys are much taller than you.'

'Ah,' said Diarmaid, 'I am taller than either of them even if the heels were off my boots' – meaning that he was better educated than they were. I haven't got any of his poetry, nor do I recall ever having heard any of it.

I knew a son of Diarmaid. His name was Seán. He had, too, I think, another son, but I didn't get to know him. Seán was a carpenter, having served his time in Ballingeary with Dónal Quill, the carpenter. Dónal was a brother of Donncha Quill, who lived in the Dirrees (in the parish of Ballyvourney).

Seán Ó Conchúir was, it seems, only a poor carpenter. Mike Beag (Sweeney) had also been apprenticed to Dónal at the same time as Seán was. Mike was a son of Tadhg Beag of Knockaunavona (in the parish of Kilgarvan in Kerry). Mike Beag, too, was only a poor carpenter.

There was a man named Con Roche who used to call around, and he had an ass. Con bargained with Mike to make him a cart-wheel. He made it, but it was crooked. The charge, I think, was fifteen shillings. Con put the wheel on the cart, and saw that it was crooked. He said he would not take it, but as he had paid some of the money in advance Mike held on to it. Mike had a couple of cows, and some time later one of them died. Con came to hear of it, 'I have heard,' he said, 'that Mike lost a cow. So,' said he, 'the wheels are turning!'

Seán Ó Conchúir went west to Kilgarvan and worked there as a carpenter. He was earning a little, and was quite good at holding on to it. He married a girl of the Buckleys; they were the Black Buckleys – the Murty Lar's who lived in Coolea. Later he became a dairyman in Inchamore (in the western part of the parish of Ballyvourney) where the Creedons now are. Before that he had had a public-house at the Crossroads, east of Kenmare. That he had to give up, and it was then he went dairying. He happened to need a man to act for him as steward, and he wrote to a gentleman in Kenmare. He sent him a man, and that man was a grandson of Daniel O'Connell of Derrynane.

Seán Ó Conchúir had a family. I knew a son and a daughter of his. They are still over west. The son was a shoemaker, and he lived in Kenmare. I presume he is still there.

Seán was much older than me. It was he who made for me my first crutch. He made it a sort of way; I'd have made it better myself! But my father was responsible. Seán was a relation of his, and it would never do to have gone to any other carpenter.

My grandfather left Coolavohir and went over west to Knock-aruddig (in the parish of Kilgarvan). There he got a farm from the landlord. Later he went to Gulba, west of Kilgarvan, and from there he went to Knockrour (also in the parish of Kilgarvan). There he stayed. He gave the land to one of his daughters, and she married Dónal O'Reilly. The sons went off to make-do for themselves.

My grandfather had, I think, four sons and three daughters. One of the girls got married above in Kilgarvan to Dónal O'Reilly. They had four daughters and four sons. The eldest son married on the land, but he didn't live long. His name was John. He directed that his share should be given to his wife; she was one of the Downeys. She was given some money and she left the place. She remarried later. The land was then given to another brother. His name was Pádraig O'Reilly. A sister of his married one of the Harringtons. Another married Séamus Lehane of Droumateuke (in the parish of Kenmare). Two others of the girls went to America. There was in that family too my father's brother, Donncha. He married Elean Murnane near Kilgarvan. A sister of hers married a man of the O'Sullivans of Corraglass, below Morley's Bridge (in the parish of Kilgarvan). She had two sons – Diarmaid, who married in the land, and Seán, who married a girl of the O'Sullivans west of Mangerton. I also had another uncle – Diarmaid Buckley, who went to America. There was also another sister, and she married Tomás Healy in Rosseeghteragh (in the parish of Kilgarvan). There was also another brother, Donncha Buckley. He, too, went to America.

My father took on dairying. His name was Pádraig Buckley. He was at that first in a place called Ucht (in the parish of Kilgarvan). There he spent seven or eight years. Then he moved over to Lounihan (also in the parish of Kilgarvan). There he acquired a farm, having come to an arrangement with the man who owned it, but who had got broken there. About £50, I think, he gave him. He also had to pay up to a £100 to the landlord; that was the amount of rent which was due.

My mother was one of the Healy Seamhrachs. 'The Seamhrachs from Laune-side,' as Diarmaid Seamhrach used to say. On one occasion they went over to the Laune to play a hurling match. They went there to play the Laune-siders, and when they were winning the others gathered stones and pelted them at them. Both sides then attacked each other, and the Stocky Connors were there.

One day later on Diarmaid Seamhrach was at Kenmare fair, and one of the Laune-siders attacked him and tried to hit him. Diarmaid hit back and lifted his attacker with one whack. ''Twas the Balcaire from Laune-side who stretched the Seamhrach at Roughty-side,' said he. Others jumped in, but Diarmaid wouldn't let them lay a finger on the Balcaire. 'I am able for him,' he said; and he was. He was my mother's uncle. He was born in Glanlea (in the parish of Kilgarvan)

I had ten brothers and two sisters. Four of my brothers went to America, and my sisters also went there. Six of my brothers were older than me. A sister of mine is still alive in America, and I am here, and that is all of us who are now left. All the others are dead, God rest their souls!

I had a brother who died when only three years of age. His name was Con. Later another brother, younger than me, was also named Con. That sometimes happened, but I don't think it should. It would have been better to have got another name.

There was John and Pat and Jerry, Denis, Dan and myself, and Con and Mike and Stephen, and the two sisters – Nora and Mary. Dan went to Australia, and he died there nine years ago, in Perth. He was two years older than me. Nora is still alive in America. She was twenty years younger than me. Jerry stayed at home, and got married there. His family are still on the land, but some of them are in America.

I am the seventh successive son. I was a doctor, but I never did any doctoring. I suppose I could kill a worm, but I have never tried it for it was said that that would be unlucky.

My father remained in Lounihan, and it is there I was born. That would have been seventy-eight years ago last Christmas. How quickly the time passes, and one's life, however long, is really short.

Many there are who never went to school. I knew several who had never seen the inside of a school, but that did not leave them entirely uneducated. They could count the cows and, if at the fair, they could correctly count the money. There was very little regard for schools in those days, or for schoolmasters either.

I must have been nearly nine years of age when first I went to school. In those days no one spent more than four years at school. I didn't learn very much there, nor was it worrying me. We didn't believe there was much to be gained from the books – only waste of time. Had it not have been for the Catechism and Confirmation there would probably have been no mention of books nor of schools at the time. One couldn't get Confirmed without some knowledge of the Catechism.

When I was preparing for Confirmation there were some twenty-five others who were learning the Catechism for the same purpose. Most of these were not attending school at all, and it was in Irish that these were learning the Catechism. Some of them were up to twenty years of age, and from that down to fifteen. We, too, were learning the Catechism, but in English. There was no regard for Irish, but should one know English well he would be looked upon as a gentleman. Those knowing only Irish were regarded as being no better than fools. It was the schools that did all the harm: people were learning English in them. Had they stayed at home they would continue having had Irish, but no English. Many, however, came to have both English and Irish, but Irish was losing ground.

I remember that while going to school – myself and three brothers of mine and a sister – a strange thing happened. The school, you might say, was only a mile distance from us. We set out one morning and weren't far from home when there came towards us on the road a goat-kid. He was bleating, and we thought that he must be going astray. He stopped and wouldn't leave us, no matter what we did. He kept rubbing up against us, just like a kitten.

We turned back, and the kid followed us. At home we told what had happened. My father said the kid must have been going astray and that we had better turn him into the wood. Back we went with the kid at our heels, but he didn't follow us very far. He stopped and would go no further with us. He turned back to the house, and we followed him. My father got a rope and put it on his neck, and we then led him into the wood. There we left the rope so that we could bring it home in the evening, but that evening, when we returned, not a sign of the rope was where we had left it, nor was there any trace of the kid. Never afterwards did we get any tidings of him, nor did anyone come looking for him.

It was not long, I assure you, until we came to have cause to regret what we had done for everything turned against us. For three years we had no luck whatever; all our calves died. The neighbours heard about the kid and they all said we should not have let him go – that he would have brought us luck. When we let him go I suppose our luck went with him.

It was said that any animal coming like that would bring luck; many people would have held on to him. Even a stray dog would maybe also bring luck.

The locality was full of goats at that time. They had everyone tormented, breaking into house-gardens and crop-fields. But they had good milk which was very strong. I often milked one of them – in the morning after breakfast, or maybe before breakfast. We had them on the mountain, and each morning one of us would have to go up and milk them. That milk would be brought home. Curds and whey would then be made from the goats' milk. That milk would be boiled in a pot on the fire, and then sour milk would be mixed with it. Indeed, no fault could be found with goats' milk – hot, cold or boiled. We would have it from one end of the year to another; we would have no other.

Poor people then had no tea. The rich had it. We would have it only on Christmas night, and not again for a whole year. It would be made in an ordinary pot, for at that time there were no tea-pots. The water having been brought to the boil, the tea would be thrown into it and stirred. Then everyone would take his share and add milk and a grain of sugar. At that time if only we got enough tea we thought we would live forever. We would be looking ahead and counting the days. 'How long now until Christmas?' we would say to one another. It was thought that Christmas was almost at hand when November came. 'Seven fat weeks from November Day to Christmas,' old people used to say to us. And they were right. We often felt that the end of those seven weeks would never come.

A custom of ours, when young, was to take out a spoon and break the handle off it. We would then edge that with a stone. That was to have been our knife for Christmas, and we would not have preferred the best knife that might now be got in a shop. We would use ours for eating butter. Maybe, however, when it was discovered that the spoon had been broken and made into a knife that we would be made to pay dearly for what we had done. The stick might be played on one's back. But there was no other knife to be had, nor were there many other things either.

Then too there were then no clocks; people had to depend on the sun to tell the time. Some had sun-dials, and they were handy when the weather was fine. They are no longer in use for now there are clocks. There is no house now that hasn't got a clock.

I was well used to having potatoes, with milk and a grain of salt, and so were many others. There was nothing else to be had in the bad times, so people had no option. Things would not be at all bad while the potatoes and the milk lasted. Indeed, times were not really bad at all until the potatoes failed.

Indian meal has been available for as long as I can remember, but it wasn't to be had when the Famine came. It was then it first came here. Stirabout was made from it, and no one need have suffered from hunger or want while there was enough of that meal to be had. A pot of stirabout was really fine food, and I would be more than pleased to get it now. There is no better food, I would say. In those days too, when the Indian meal first came in, there was but very little bread to be had, nor very much oatmeal, so everyone used stirabout.

Indian meal was also given to the pigs, to the hens and to the cows, and they fattened on it. It would also fatten the human head, and who then could regard it as being poor food. People at that time worked hard, and fine healthy people they were. They weren't given to complaining as people now are.

I was about nine years of age when I lost my leg. One night I went off to bed as usual. Next morning, when I went to get up, my leg was lifeless. I was attending school at the time.

Our house was a thatched one, and I was down below in the room. There were two rooms, with the kitchen in between. Potatoes and milk we would have in the morning. My mother called me to get up – that the potatoes were ready. My little trousers were a bit away from me. I jumped out of bed, and when I did I fell. I thought that it was pins and needles that had affected my leg: I couldn't understand it. I started to cry, and my mother came to me. I had neither a pain nor an ache in my leg, but from that day to this it has been entirely lifeless. A doctor came, but there was nothing he could do for me; he had nothing to do. And that is why I went tailoring. Otherwise, I presume I would have taken to some other trade.

I was only thirteen years of age when I became apprenticed. I took up tailoring. I spent five years apprenticed in Kenmare. The apprenticeship term is still five years. One, at that time, had to get a security, and £9 would have to be paid if he failed to fully serve his time; the master could get at him.

I paid a £9 fee in the first instance. Then I had to pay another £9 for the term and work hard as well, but the worst of all was that I never got enough to eat. The mistress would cut a bit of bread, and I would have to make do with that from seven o'clock in the evening until nine o'clock next morning. I would be called at six in the morning and would then have to work until nine with nothing to eat.

While serving my time I had to be up at day-break and work until night. There would be only two meals – morning and evening. My table, I tell you, was a scanty one, and if people today had to depend on the food which I had they would, indeed, be in a bad way. There I spent five years, working without food or clothes.

I had an uncle who had a farm near Kenmare; he was my

mother's brother. While serving my time I used to visit him
every Sunday. There I would have my dinner, starving hungry as
I was. I would never have had enough during the week. Were it
not for my uncle I could hardly have survived at all, things were
really so bad.

A lot of people had very little means in those days. Some had
only the grass of a couple of cows, and that often was bad. We did
not have it that bad: we had twelve cows and a big stretch of
mountain. We had goats on the mountain as well as dry stock.
Four farmers shared that mountain, and they all could put dry
cattle on it. You, for example, could have so many collops there
and I likewise, and so on.

Had I not taken to a trade I might, perhaps, have been
struggling with a farm, or I might have gone to America as some
of my brothers did. But, I suppose, each one's destiny is laid out
for him, and perhaps it is all for the best.

Having served my time everything was then fine, except that
I had not learned to cut out. Tailors long ago had no cut. They
would have patterns and things like that. In England and other
places the tailors had got the cut long before it came to Ireland,
but even after it had come here one could not get it from the
tailor with whom he served his time. He would have to go to
some other tailor to learn it, and then pay dearly for it. Anyone
wishing to learn the cut had to go to a tailor who had it, spend
six months with him, pay him a trifle, and learn the cut from
him.

But I hadn't got the cut. I set out and went to work in
Killarney, in Tralee, in Mallow and in Cork. I spent fourteen
years in that city, and a while in Youghal. I then went to
Scotland, and spent three years there. I then came to Dublin and
spent six months there. After that I returned to Cork and spent
another while there. It was from a tailor in Cork – Sugrue – that
I learned the cut.

In Cork I spent six months learning the cut. The master paid
me a certain amount a week, depending on the amount of work
I would do. I used to spend two hours a day learning the cut. What
I was paid gave me sufficient to pay for my lodgings – nine
shillings a week.

It is said that a rolling stone gathers no moss. The years were catching up on me and so I thought I had better do something for myself and, save the mark! as Jerry Coakley used to say, I came here and married a woman of the McCarthys. That was thirty-nine years ago. I have been here ever since. I have liked the place and got on well there. I have two sons. One of them is in Cork and the other here at home. An acre of land is what we have here.

Times were bad when I came here and it was hard to make money but, by God, if the times were then bad they are much worse now. We had hoped that things would improve sooner or later. The food has improved. Food is good now, but there is no longer as much work available as there used to be. No one is any longer prepared to work. No one now who would do any hard work. No fear that people now would strain themselves. Times are still bad, and always will be, I suppose.

2. *The Famine and the Bad Times*

The Famine continued on for two or three years, but it was in its first year that most people died. The potatoes had got blighted, a thing that had never previously happened. People had been almost entirely dependent on the potatoes; they had no other food, except oatmeal and stirabout for part of the winter. Had there been anyone to do something for them when the potatoes failed they might not have died as they did; food was plentiful in other countries. No call went out to those countries; the English, I suppose, would not have permitted it. They only wanted people to die so that they could get the place for themselves.

By and large, it was not at all of starvation that people died but of the sickness and of the disease that came in its train. People used to say that the starvation was in the air, and there was disease in the air as well. Sickness was in the wind; it always comes with famine. Later, should the people get something to eat, they would then go out, fall, and die. The food would have been too strong for them in their utter state of starvation.

When the potatoes failed people ate turnips. These would have been by no means poor food had there been enough of them. They would, at least, have kept the people alive. But the turnips did not last long. People went into the fields and stole them and ate them uncooked, starving as they were. Then the turnips killed them. Soon too neither turnips nor potatoes were to be had, and any corn that was in the country was being sent over to England.

The people then used to dig up dock-roots and eat them, and they also cooked and ate dandelions. They also ate nettles while they lasted. Dandelions, if cooked, could be just as good as cabbage.

People also killed crows and ate them. Even the crows were weak, for hunger had caught them too when the potatoes failed. A nice young crow could make good food, but an old crow is useless. Anyhow, they too were also eaten.

Hundreds had died before relief came. The Indian meal came from the Russians – when first it ever came to Ireland. People knew nothing about it, nor of the making of Indian meal stirabout. They had no idea as to how it should be used. They tried to make the stirabout, but some made it too thin and others too thick, and so it was for a long time. It would have been better thin than thick at the time, for if it had been too thick it would have been over-strong, and any over-strong food would have killed the people. But they really knew nothing about it, and often it was not sufficiently boiled. Indian meal needs to be well boiled; it could never be over-cooked.

In some places sheds were built in the fields and boilers were installed to make gruel for poor people. Even with these the poor were often unfairly treated. Had they been given sufficient gruel they would not have died as they did. All the laws in those days were unjust; no law favoured the poor.

There were no workhouses when the Famine came. It was later that they were built, but people felt ashamed to go into them. They would rather die outside, and so, too, they did.

North in Coolea gruel was being made. There was a boiler in Alackagh. A man was in charge, doling out the gruel to poor people. He was hunchbacked. Years later the old Tailor Crowley was working in Coolea. Four or five lads from the neighbourhood, who were present, were poking fun at him. He was on the table working. A son of the man who used to be giving out the gruel was the chief fun-poker. Something he said really annoyed the tailor, and he replied:

Can you recall the year in Alackagh,
The time of the gruel and the rations?
That's what put the huge hump on your father –
Scraping and stirring the boiler.

He let on that that was what had caused the hump on the old man.

Often I heard my mother, God rest her soul! tell of people who called, in an utter state of collapse from hunger. They would be given some food and then they would go out. Outside they would fall dead, God bless the hearers! They would, it seems, have over-eaten, or the food might have been too strong for them. Often they were buried where they had fallen.

In a field-corner at the foot of Mangerton there is a grave. The place is named Crossmount. Someone who had died during the Famine had been buried there. And on the roadside near

Kilgarvan there is a cross named Cormac Óg's Cross. It is there he is buried. I don't know who he was, but I have been told that it was in the year of the Famine he was buried. He died of hunger. There is a crossroads there. I don't know of any place here in Ballingeary where anyone like that was buried except in the graveyard in Gougane. I know that some like that were buried there.

To the west of Kenmare there is a place where a big wide grave was made. People were brought there in carts, dead, and buried all together and the clay thrown over them, coffinless. So many were dying that it was impossible to provide coffins for them. It was quite common to see a man carrying a corpse on his back, taking it to the graveyard for burial. Men in those days were really strong, if only they had food. I have heard, too, of a woman who took on her back her husband who had died and buried him in the graveyard – herself.

I am convinced that at that time some were buried who were not dead at all. It was that they had collapsed from hunger and lay back as if they were dead. I have heard of some who regained consciousness as they were being taken to the graveyard, or as they were being put into the grave.

Due to the vast number of deaths and the prevailing starvation, the parish priest of Kilgarvan had only two baptisms in the year of the Famine and the following year. Still many survived.

There had been fine potato crops before the Famine. Potatoes were planted everywhere. Look at any hill-side and you will see there ridge-traces. People had grubbed and dug and burned the scraws and had then used that as a fertiliser for the potatoes.

I have heard of two crops of potatoes being grown in a field some years. Often potatoes were set in the beginning of June – the land having been grubbed and burnt, and the ashes having been laid on as fertiliser. From that fine crops of Black Minions would be produced. They, I have been told, were excellent potatoes. I have never seen them, but I think they were there when the blight came. I have seen later on another sort – Black Apples. They were tip-top. They were well-coloured – a sort of red. Then came the Red Quarries, and they too were good. They would be set around St Patrick's Day and dug in July. I don't think there were any other really good potatoes round the time of the Famine. It was later that they came. The Black Apples and the Quarries have long since disappeared, too.

Then, after the Famine, it was common practice to get a quill,

cut off both its ends, and then use it to take out the potato- eye.
That was the sceallán or potato set. Very little of the potato
would be wasted in that way. What was taken out would be set
and the rest eaten, and, by Jove, what was set grew. How
extraordinary! And I have heard that they grew well.

Before the blight first hit the potato stalks would stay green
up to Christmas. A ridge of two of them would have been left in
the ground, and it was then they would be dug. The stalks would
still be as green as they would have been in the autumn.

The potatoes were of very poor quality in the year 1880. That
year they were entirely water. They had been struck by the
blight and left utterly useless as food. Also they were very small.

Then, the following year, the Champions came. They were
excellent potatoes, and grand to eat. They were the best potatoes
ever. They are still to be had in places and hard to beat.

Somehow, all the other potato varieties had failed by that
time. All potatoes are good at first, but they deteriorate later on.
It would be advisable to rotate them or have them changed from
one place to another. Potatoes grown in bogland or in peaty soil
would then thrive well in other soils. They would benefit from
the change.

In the year 1880 there was a man who had seven in family. His
potatoes were so small that he would be hard put to have dug
enough for the dinner after his breakfast. Unless he hurried hard
the dinner wouldn't be ready until nightfall. Having eaten his
dinner he would have to be off again so that he could have dug
enough for another meal before suppertime. He would be in such
a hurry eating them that he wouldn't peel them at all.

One day, while having his dinner, he looked out the window
and saw that his neighbour's cows had got into a field of first-
crop grass. Out he went and called the neighbour. He informed
him that the cows were in the first-crop grass. Having told him
that he took the potatoes out of his mouth, and when he counted
them he found that he had had together in his mouth nine
potatoes!

Another day that man had a meitheal digging the potatoes,
and they were very small. He had in his pocket a gold half-
sovereign, wherever he had got it, and by Jove, he was afraid he
might lose it. Out from the ridge hopped a fairly large potato. He
got a knife and cut a gash in the potato and put the half-sovereign

– the Grasshopper, as it used to be called – into it. He then laid the potato on the top of a rock. A crow came and snatched it off. In full cry, they all set out after the crow and spent the entire day chasing the crow until eventually they got the potato off him. That's how they spent the day, getting but very little else done before evening.

In those days, there would have been a quern in every house with which corn was ground in winter-time. Gruel would be made from the oatmeal, and good food that was. White cabbage would be cut up and cooked in the gruel, along with the oatmeal. Left over there might have been the bones of an old cow, and they would have been really good for the gruel-making. No milk was available in winter, but the gruel was a good substitute.

About the end of May, or early in June, when the potatoes had all been used up, and next year's potatoes set, those who had hill-land, extending from what was arable, would take the cows up there. They might also have a couple of goats or more. Beside a rock, up in the hill, a little house would have been built, roofed with scraws. There they would make butter. Also they would boil the goats' milk and crack it so as to make curds and whey.

The skin would be stripped off rushes and cores kept. Then a certain amount of blood – about a quart – would be drawn with lances from the dry stock. From the neck of each animal the blood would be drawn. Then the rush-cores would, with the blood, be put into a pot, so as to make it firm. It would become like a cake. Criss-cross the rush-cores would have been put in with the blood. The lot would then be boiled, taken up, and put aside for it to set. That, then, would be eaten with the curds, and that's how they lived on the hill during the summer. There would be no potatoes to be had at that time of the year.

Up there they would remain until about mid-July, when they would come back down again. Potatoes from then on would again be coming available, and cabbage too. The cabbage would be chopped up, and salt and sour skimmed milk added. That would be used as a dressing for the potatoes. It would be hard to find fault with it. It was better than nothing, but it would never do now.

In Limerick, that was commonly given to the wandering labourers who went there for the potato-digging. They would have it regularly for their supper, and would be given neither a fork nor spoon; they had only to stick their fingers into the plate and eat away.

Milk was very scarce in those days. The really bad times were over in my youth, but times were still bad. People, in winter, would have a firkin, and into that they would strain, morning and evening, whatever little milk they had, or perhaps only once a day, depending on the amount of milk they might have.

At the base of the firkin there would be a hole with plug stuck in it. That plug could be pulled out and the milk, as required, drained off. That's what was done. It was simple. Further milk would continue to be added, and then it would be put all together into the churn and butter made from whatever cream there might be. That butter would be pickled by dissolving a grain of salt in a basin and adding that to the butter.

In every house there would be a crock – a large earthenware crock. Some of those crocks are still left. Into the crock the butter would be put and left there for maybe three months, awaiting the going to Cork. I might have a half-firkin, and you the same. Both our butter-shares would be sent off to Cork – all in the one firkin. Then, later when the money came it would be equally divided. People in those days were in some ways very astute, but not in other ways.

In those days, too, there were no ploughs; it was all spade-work. Hard and slow that work was, but there was no alternative. People, too, would draw the manure on their backs – in wicker baskets. Then times changed. Wooden ploughs came to be made. It was carpenters, of course, who made them. A blacksmith would make the iron sock. At first, of course, there were no good ploughmen, due to lack of experience.

In Kerry there happened to be two men who got themselves a wooden plough. Each paid his share. They set to work, intending to plough a field for potatoes. To the plough they yoked a pair of horses. Tomás was the horse-guide and Tadhg the ploughman. They ploughed up a sod, right down to the lower end of the field. So pre-occupied were they with their work that it never occurred to them to look back and see how they had been faring until they got right down to the very end. When eventually they did look back, there was their sod having fallen back into the furrow. 'Never mind,' said Tomás, 'one must spoil while learning to spin!' However, they improved. They found out that they had not been properly working the plough.

A man named Seán O'Donoghue was mowing hay, being given only stirabout to eat three times a day. He was a hired man and the stirabout he was given was very thin. On a Sunday morning he was to go to Mass. The housewife came and turned the stirabout out into a dish. By Jove, it ran around the dish. 'Lord save us,' said Seán, 'it will surely catch up with first Mass in Limerick!'

None thought of going off to the other countries before the Famine. They all stayed at home, and so the country became over-populated. After the Famine, however, as they had nothing to live on, they started to move off. It was in the years following 1880 that the awful emigration took place. An odd one had gone off previously, but then they all went, and, for twenty years, they kept going non-stop. Those still at home would be only waiting for the money to pay their passage-fares.

To America they mostly went. Quite a number, too, went to Australia, but the vast majority went to America. For every hundred who went to America only about ten went to Australia and other countries. It was easy, at the time, to earn a living in America. And it was the best – all the young strong men – who went. Had I the use of my leg, I, too, would probably have gone, as I had brothers and sisters who went to America. Anyone with a defect of any sort had to stay here.

In those days, those going to America would each take aboard a sack of potatoes, a sack of cabbage, and perhaps some fish. Very little meat was to be had at that time. Each one could also take some butter. There were some, too, who took with them a goat – a milch goat – for her milk. It is said, too, that that's how the first goat got to America – from Ireland. Before that there were no goats over there, but the place filled up with them later on. Then, I dare say, they would have been glad to be again rid of them for the goat is a devil that is impossible to control.

Going to America at that time people had a three-month sea journey. The ships then were very slow, and the wind might put them off course. It was white cabbage that people took with them; green cabbage would have been too hard to cook. Unlike today, no food would be available aboard ship, nor any other necessities, as they are now.

There were many married people who went to America. I knew a man who had a wife and family when going there. They opted to set out and try to make a living out there rather than be struggling with life here. They went off leaving behind them the terrible times that were here. There were no bad times in America. Work was to be had – hard work – but those people were strong and wouldn't grumble about having to work.

There was another thing, too, that I noticed, and it surprised me. There were many whom I knew who at that time went off to America not knowing a word of English, any more than would the cat! Irish was their only language, just like all before them. And isn't it extraordinary that they got on well over beyond, just as good as if they had known English when going there. Somehow or other they picked up English.

Con Scannell went to America. He was a native of Inchamore (in the western part of the parish of Ballyvourney). He had a wife and children. By Jove, having got over, he set out in search of work. Travelling along he got lost. He couldn't find his way back. The poor devil who had only a couple of words of English! He met a man, but he had no Irish. He realised, however, that Con had gone astray. He asked him where he lived, and this is how Con replied: 'Con Scannell, one wife, one child. The Little Cord Road, Rockstone'. Rockstone was the name of the place from where he had set out, and there was there a wire telegraph along the road outside the house. Con had no idea what that was, but he called the street Little Cord Road.

I also knew a man of the Burkes from Ballingeary who went to America, and he, too, hadn't a word of English when he left here. He returned years later knowing English and, better still, he had made a lot of money. There are some who would say that Irish is useless when one leaves Ireland, and that he couldn't successfully emigrate without knowing English. Don't believe them; there are many who went off knowing no English and later made a pile of money. This man of the Burkes returned again to America.

There was also another thing. Farmers were very hard on their servant boys. They treated them wretchedly. For a long time all they would get from any farmer was their grub and clothing, having spent a whole year working. There were even farmers who would grumble for having to give even that much. Many of the farmers were utter tyrants. They were snobbish, and they robbed the poor people.

There was one of the Cronins who lived in Gorteenakilla

(north of Ballingeary) and his potatoes ran out before the new ones came in. Each day a cake of bread was baked for the men. (He had at that time working for him two girls and three boys.) They all failed to eat the cake. They left it untouched. With nothing else to eat, they had to go without food that day.

That cake was once more put out on the table at supper-time, but not a bit of it was touched. Again, next day, they were given the same cake, and milk too. They drank the milk and left the cake. Still again they were given it for their dinner.

One of the boys was a cow-herd. His name was Seán Óg Creed. The others, between them, put together five pence and offered it to the cow-boy if only he would take the cake and bury it or get rid of it somewhere where it would never again be found. Seán Óg stole the cake and buried it. However, he was suspected of having taken it. The man of the house attacked him for what he had done; he had got tipped off by one of the girls. Seán ran away and went home, but he got beaten again when he got home for having left his job. He got no sympathy.

He then went to work with James Kelleher in Gortafluddig (south-east of Gougane Barra). James was a farmer, and Seán Óg spent twenty years working for him. By that time he had saved up a bit of money, and he got married.

Now, regarding the Cronins: they, later on, fell into dire poverty, and some of them died. They had got heavily into debt and the land had to be sold, so that's what they gained from the cake. They had been over-greedy, but that was the luckless greed.

A halfpenny in olden times was worth a lot. It is not worth much now. There was once a weaver whose son was all set to go to the Whitsun in Ballyvourney on a Whit Sunday. Of course, he needed money. By Jove, his father gave him tuppence. 'Here,' he said, 'break up that' – meaning that he should spend it. Of course, tuppence wasn't all that bad at the time. It would relieve one's hunger, or his thirst!

The old age pension was only a crown when first it was granted. Denis Lynch of Darragh (north-east of Ballingeary) had a brother who was getting the pension. One day, at Macroom fair, he met this brother. 'Well,' said the brother, 'is it long more until you'll get crowned?' – meaning if it was long until he, too, would be getting the pension.

The pension then went up to seven and six pence, and later a further half-crown was added. That meant a lot to poor people who were growing old without a livelihood, and there is no regard for anyone who hasn't got a bit of money, nor is he shown much respect.

Old people were really to be pitied before the pension came. Many of them had to set out on their own and take to begging throughout the country at the end of their days. It was a hard life. I knew many of them – respectable people who were forced to travel in the hope of getting a bite here and a bite there. Their families would have gone off to America, or somewhere else, and so they would have had no one left.

3. *Some Personal Memoirs*

I remember when first I went to Cork things were very cheap. Beef and mutton would cost only sixpence a pound, and a measure of potatoes only the same, I think. Also, unlike now, rents were by no means heavy; houses in the city which would then cost only from a pound to thirty shillings would now cost three pounds or more. Times have utterly changed, getting worse every day. A £100 wouldn't go very far now.

The first matches I ever saw were called Tally-ho Matches. Three boxes of those could be had for a penny when first they came. People wondered at them for prior to that they had only the flint.

A farmer out ploughing in a field, or at any other work, would take out with him a sod of turf and a live coal. He would place them beside the fence, and whenever he wanted to have a smoke he had only to go to the coal. People then thought that things were great when the matches came. They were really wonderful.

Previous to that, should the fire go out, one had to go to a neighbour's house and get a live coal to re-kindle the fire. I often saw that happen.

Very little tobacco was being smoked when I was a boy. Often, at that time, I saw a man – the man of the house, the old man – who would be smoking, and if he had a son he too might be smoking, but if he were it was unknown to his father. It didn't matter how old or young that son might be – whether twenty or forty years of age – he wouldn't smoke in front of his father. I saw that happen as often as I have got fingers on me. I have also seen a man who was married, with a wife and family, and while his father lived he never smoked in his presence, nor would he let on that he smoked at all. The old man lived to be over eighty, and his son would then have been over forty and having a family of his own.

I saw others too who never smoked while their old people lived. Tobacco was then scarce, and pipes too were scarce. Only clay pipes were then to be had. The pipe which the old man had would be that which his son would then have after his death. I have seen many, too, who never smoked at all until after their fathers' death, and they might then be up to forty years of age. I assure you that in those days people knew how properly to behave.

When a priest came to hold a station in a house everyone felt afraid of him. No one would smoke in his presence. That I have also seen happen. Should some of them feel like having a smoke out they would go and have their smoke in a field-corner. The priest wouldn't have liked them to smoke in his presence. Many of the priests were like that, but I dare say they too smoked just like others.

Cheap tobacco was to be had from hucksters who called to collect eggs. They would have a basket lined with straw, and tobacco too. A finger-length of tobacco could be bought from them. That was the measure – a middle finger-length. That, too, was the way yards were measured at that time – exactly seven finger-lengths to the yard. The finger-length of tobacco was hoop-shaped. Rat-tail that tobacco was called. Anyone smoking at that time would have sufficient for a month in an ounce of tobacco. People then didn't smoke very much. People smoking today would smoke six times as much as they did.

When a stranger called to a house the pipe would be lighted up for him, as a novelty. There were very few other novelties at the time. The stranger would then have a smoke, and so would any others who might be present. The pipe would be handed round so that each one would pray for the dead. That was a custom of the time, but that custom has now almost completely died out.

At that time, too, a box of clay pipes would be brought to every wake-house. They would cost only a halfpenny each, and could be had for even less when bought in bulk. Some tobacco would also be provided. The pipes would be filled with tobacco and one would be given to each smoker. Quite often some might get two or three pipes each. The smoker having smoked his pipe would then put it in his pocket. A little later someone could again come around with a plate-full of the clay pipes. Anyone who had pocketed the first one might then take another. Then, surely, he would have so many that he had no need to buy any at all for himself. There would, of course, be another wake later on.

Even the women would be given a clay pipe filled with tobacco. That was the custom; no distinction was made between the men and the women. Each woman would light up her pipe, but she might take only one puff of it, but they all prayed for the dead, and that's what it was all about.

When a pipe got empty it was refilled again and again. The plate would come round – up to twenty times in the course of the night.

There are now no clay pipes. I haven't seen one for years. However, should you happen to be ploughing a field for potatoes you might, and quite often, come across the bowl of an old clay pipe. It must at some time have got out with the manure.

I was here one evening fixing up a little patch of cabbage which I had. A gentleman strolled down to me, from Gougane. He was a stranger who was on holidays. He had in his mouth a really fine pipe. He sat in front of me on the fence, and we chatted. Having smoked the pipe he laid it on the fence. A little while later he went back home. I, too, went on home.

Night fell, but it wasn't long until he arrived back with his tongue hanging out. He had lost the pipe. We went out to search for it. I knew where exactly on the fence he had been seated, and so did he. By God, we failed to find it, high or low. I said I would search again in the morning.

Out I went again next morning, and searched, but I failed to find the pipe, nor any trace of it. So matters rested. In the evening I went out again to tidy up my cabbage-patch. I got up on the fence and there, on the fence, was the pipe – exactly where the gentleman had left it. I found it there without searching at all for it.

As sure as you are where you are that pipe must have been in some way enchanted, for it had not been there in the morning. It could not have been there unknown to me; but how did it come to be there in the evening, or where had it been?

I remember a place where there was the ruins of an old house. It had been a thatched house, and it must have been a couple of hundred years since it was built. It was knocked down; the stones were needed to build a new house. In the corner of the house-ruins, under the foundation stone, was found a clay pipe filled with tobacco and a cover on it.

It was customary in olden times when a new house was being built to place something under the foundation stone. Those who were well off would put there a coin. Why it was done I do not know.

I remember seeing keeners when I was very young. These were women. They would come to every wake. As soon as they arrived they would, first of all, weep aloud, and then they would keen. That keen would be all in Irish.

There was no regard for anyone who would not have a keener when one of his household died. It was the custom and everyone felt compelled to have one. A half-crown, I think, was the payment given to the keeners. That, at the time, was good money. It was better than £1 today, and it would go further.

There were men, too, who composed keens, and they were poets, but somehow it was women mainly who did the keening. They would come to the wake and keen and cry. They would cry over a corpse, no matter who the dead person was. They needn't be in any way related to the deceased, but still one would imagine that their hearts were broken. That was a gift they had, for indeed it was gift. Not everyone could keen, never mind the poetry.

On the day of the funeral they would again attend. They would lead the funeral, constantly keening – praising the deceased and declaring that there had been no one better and what a tragedy that death had been. I dare say they wouldn't at all have meant it, but what matter when they had got their pay.

By God, those times are now gone. Should anyone nowadays be offered £20 to compose a keen he wouldn't be able to earn the money. Poetry is a thing of the past, and so are the keeners. There is very little weeping now to be heard at any wake.

I saw, too, how farmers were circumstanced at that time. My own people were farmers. They would be up before sunrise in the morning and work hard until night again fell. They kept constantly on the trot and still never seemed to get to the end of what there was to be done.

Everyone's life was hard as well as that of the farmers. The tradesman's life was hard for their pay was poor. Also they didn't have the work-conveniences that tradesmen now have. The tailor, for example, had no sewing machine; he had to sew by hand with a needle. Of frieze mostly a suit of clothes would be made in those days. That was a strong, thick cloth, and difficult to sew. One would have a pain in his hand, right up to the shoulder, having spent a day on the table sewing.

The machines – the sewing machines – however brought a great change, and the frieze came to be replaced by other cloths. They were light and easy to sew. So it is today with the lighter cloths, but they are of poor quality. They would keep out neither rain nor cold. They are but poor shelter in winter-time. They are really only rags. Were the old people of forty years ago still alive they would have less regard for that cloth than they should for a dog, nor would they wear it at all. They had been accustomed to the frieze, and no other cloth was as good as that nor as long-wearing. Frieze would last for twenty years, and still be good – better than any of the cloths now to be had in the shops. It was utter folly to have discarded the frieze.

The frieze was really great cloth. It lasted well. I have seen a frieze coat which lasted for twenty years and more. I have also seen a piece of it which had been in use for even thirty years; a coat had been made of it. There is no cloth now even half as good. It was a good shelterer; it would let in neither rain nor cold.

Forty years ago I saw an overcoat which had been made of frieze. It was sent to Cork to be dyed. Well, the man who owned that coat would have got £8 for it, into his hand, from a schoolmaster, the first day he walked out wearing it but, indeed, he wouldn't accept it. He wouldn't have sold that coat for any money.

That coat lasted from time to time and from year to year, and I know it is still in the house. The cloth never wore out. He failed to wear it out; the frieze was too good. Eventually that coat ripped apart when the thread with which it had been sewn wore out. He had intended to get a tailor to re-sew it, but he didn't. Had he done so he would still have that coat. He could have remained unconcerned about either cold or harsh weather while he should have it. Even he used to wear that coat when drawing lime. The lime would have ruined any other coat – it would have burned the cloth – but the frieze was too strong.

Frieze and flannel would be made up into bales. Often up to sixty bundles would be in the bale, depending on how many there would be in a household. Not always would the same amount be in a bale.

Before the people took to making flannel and frieze at home there was, in every parish, a man – the dyer – and he, I think, was being paid by the government. He would call to each house and be given a certain amount of wool – so many pounds – according to the size of the household. The dyer's pound was the equivalent of three small pounds – three times as much as today's pound. He would have a scales – iron scales – and would weigh out a certain number of pounds. That would then have to be warped, and when it was spun and warped the dyer would then come along again and take it to the weaver.

In the case of those who lived away out in the hills the weaver would come along with his ass. He would have an apprentice. The weaver himself would travel out maybe two days a week and the apprentice two other days – collecting the yarns. On the ass there would be two sacks attached like a pannier-stradle – one on each side.

Back at Incheese Bridge (in the parish of Kilgarvan) there was a man named Seán Léan Dinneen. His mother happened to need dye to dye some flannel. At home the dyeing was done at the time. She told Seán to go to Macroom for the dye; it wasn't to be had anywhere nearer. 'What sort?' he asked. 'Brown,' she told him, 'copperas and longwood.'

She gave Seán the price of the dye and sixpence for expenses, and he set off for Macroom. He liked a drop, and in Macroom he met a friend. They went off together to have a drink. Seán, in the event, spent whatever money he had and had nothing left with which to buy the dye. Not being acquainted with any of the shopkeepers he had to head back for home without the dye.

It was late when he got home, and he went off to bed. His mother got up in the morning and called him. 'Anything to tell after the night?' she inquired.

'Nothing,' said Seán, 'but something you might find hard to believe.'

'And what might that be?' said she.

'That the colour of the drink,' said he, 'was better than that of the copperas; so that was the dye I brought home.'

There were some very droll people in those days who often said the most comical things. Anyhow, the mother had no option but to send someone else for the dye.

Previous to that rock-mould and camomile and moss were used

for dyeing. The mould was a hard substance to be found on the side of rocks, and had to be scraped off. All three were boiled together and the water then strained off. The flannel would be put into that water and again boiled. That would make a grand brown or russet dye, and cloth would hold that colour, unfaded, for twenty years.

For the dyeing of flannel black, or dark blue, people went to the black pit and brought home the black in a can. That was to be found in a bog, and nowhere else, but not in every bog. There was only one place here where it was – in Gortafluddig. Pouladiff – the black pit – was there, and it is still there.

That black is soft and soggy, and people who went to get it always had a horse-shoe in the can to ensure that it stayed active. The wind and the air would render is useless. Iron would keep it from going dead. Perhaps there was some iron nature in the ground where it was to be found. Anyhow, it was used to dye flannel dark blue, and a grand, fast dye it was. Frocks were made from the flannel, and men's coats too.

The black would be put, with a drop of water, into a pot, and boiled. Into that, then, the flannel would be put and left there for four hours or more. Then it would be taken out and washed in clean, cold water, and it would then be dark blue. There was no need to mix anything with it – only itself and the water.

Other than those I saw nothing else being used until copperas and longwood came in. They were to be had in the shops, but they were in no way as good as the older dyes.

Carmen, in those days, took the butter to Cork and by God, a man named Lucey set up a dye-house in Cork city. He, I think, had come to Cork from Ballyvourney. People then started sending the flannel to Cork to get it dyed, and that put an end to the home-dyeing. A bale of flannel would be sent to Cork, and that would suffice for quite a while.

There was here a woman who wanted to send a bale of flannel to Cork for dyeing. A carman was to take it. 'What colour do you want?' said he. 'The colour of the needle-paper,' said she. Needles, at that time, came in a slate-coloured paper. I think the colour is still the same.

Waxed thread for shoemakers was being made before ever it could be bought in any shop. It was being made at home. The shoemaker, in those days, came to the house, just as the tailor did. While he would be making the shoes the housewife would be spinning flax to make thread out of it. With a potato and a spindle she would make the thread, in the same way as the thread for the tailor.

A raw potato and a spindle was what was used for the spinning. The potato would be placed on the top of the spindle and the flax tied beneath it. A strand of the thread would be attached at the top. The flax would be held in the left hand and the spindle turned with the other, and the potato would spin around. The flax would be constantly payed out. The woman spinner would be up on something high so that the thread would fall well down from her while spinning. That thread could be as fine or as thick as was desired, depending on the way it was fed.

Women, in the same way, made thread for the tailors. That thread was made from wool, and dyed. That's all now a thing of the past. The other thread then became available, and it was easier to buy it than to be making it. Indeed, I could still make thread – for a shoemaker or for a tailor – with a potato and a spindle, and I doubt if there is anyone else around who could.

When the flax was being prepared the tow, first of all, had to be removed from it. It would all then be of equal quality. The flax having been in that way haffled, it could all be then made into thread, should one so desire.

Regarding the bark of the flax – the coarse tow – that too had to be removed. To do that it had to be beaten on hard ground with a mallet and then made up into small sheaves – into little rolls – folded into plaits.

The haffling would have removed the tow. That tow would then be sprinkled under the yarn when the cloth was being made – cast under the yarn as stiffening.

Flour, in olden times, was cheap. A twenty-stone sack of flour was to be had for thirty shillings. It then went up to £2. Prior to that a lot of Indian meal was being used, and that was very nourishing. Then the tea came in, as well as flour for baking and bread-making.

Flour, when it first came in, was very scarce. No one would get more than a hundredweight and would have to make do with that for a whole year. It came in firkins in those days – before sacks became available. It happened like this: butter was being sent to the market in Cork; a carter would be going there. I might have a firkin of butter and you two firkins. The firkins would be empty for the return journey so the flour would be filled into them in Cork for the carter to take with him. A hundredweight of flour would be the fill of a firkin. That's the way it worked over sixty years ago.

We had a craving for bread, and should we get a chunk of it we would have been more than satisfied. Tea, too, was very scarce, and we very rarely had it. Should we have been able to get the bread we wouldn't have minded about the tea.

The white flour, I think, did more harm than good. I remember the fine strong teeth which old people then had; that's when they had the Indian meal and the stirabout. They were all stout and strong and well-nourished, and in good health. Later, having taken to the flour, their teeth rotted and failed. They would have toothache, and other aches too. So it is ever since.

People came to the conclusion that something was being mixed with the flour, to whiten it. I have heard it said that chalk was being mixed with the flour, and I would be inclined to agree.

In olden times people had a bread-stand for baking; there were no bastables at the time. Under the bread-stand, which was a fairly wide board, there were four legs. It would be sloped slightly backwards. On it, in front of the fire, would be placed the cake, and it would bake handsomely. However, the cake would have to be turned when one side was baked. That would be as good as any bastable cake.

The bread-stand was made entirely of wood, and it could be raised or lowered as desired by moving the legs in or out. These bread-stands have long since gone out of use.

Fifty years ago there were people who went around selling tea. They would have a horse and van, and they were to be found travelling everywhere. They would call to every house and might spend a whole hour urging that the tea should be bought. It would have been better to buy it than to be arguing with them, and easier. Anyhow, they wouldn't leave until they had one fully tormented. They might be asked if the tea was good and, of course, they would say that there was none better, and that it was for nothing at a half-crown a pound.

Tea, when it first came in, was being so highly praised that everyone bought it. Then it needn't be paid for there and then.

The tea-men preferred that it wouldn't, for that would have been a good excuse for their calling again. That tea, however, was by no means good.

Listening to people at that time was really laughable. They talked of nothing else but tea – how it should be made and drawn, and how milk and sugar should be added. Anyone on a night-visit to a neighbour's house, or calling in for some reason in the day time, wouldn't be let go until he had a cup of tea – just to find out if it in anyway differed from the tea which that person had got.

In no two houses would the tea be the same. It might not have been made in the same way, nor might the water have been the same. That could make a difference, for waters differ. There is good water and bad – bog-water and clear spring water. Water with a bog-taste is by no means good. Being heavy it is impossible to make good tea with it. It is sour and soft.

For the drawing of the tea there was at that time a tea-drawer. People thought that unless it was drawn in the tea-drawer it wouldn't be properly drawn at all. There are now no tea-drawers – only tea-pots – but when the tea was drawn in the tea-drawer it was then it would be put into the pot.

People thought that cups and saucers were great when first they came in – the way they were made. I presume they had not anything previously made of the same stuff. There had been only wooden vessels in olden times – wooden piggins and mugs.

There happened to be a woman who somehow found a cup and saucer, which she brought home. These aroused great curiosity. A friend of hers called in one day and she wanted to show off with her cup and saucer. She took them out and poured tea into the cup. Tea was rare then, too. She gave her friend the tea, and he sat by the fire. He took hold of the cup, but didn't grip the saucer. The saucer fell to the floor and got smashed into smithereens. He let on to have been startled and said that he thought that the saucer had been attached to the cup – that he thought it was a trencher. Of course, he was only joking, for he had often previously seen a cup and saucer, and had tea out of them.

Lots of things were scarce, and people had very little education. When anything new came in it took them a long time to learn how it should be used. Take the clock, for instance: clocks were to be found only in the houses of the gentry. In the beginning people thought there must have been something magical about a clock and the way it would show the time at any hour of the day or night. Then came the watches and people said that they were more wonderful still – it being possible to carry them wherever one liked, in the pocket.

There was a man in this district who got himself a big clock. That must have been sixty years ago or more. He put it hanging on the wall. A clock like that was to be had for ten shillings, I think, and there is no clock now that would be half as good as they were. The right stuff was then being put into them, unlike the clocks of today. These would last only a few years.

Anyhow, everyone was coming to see this clock and wondering what time it would show. An educated man, of course, could tell the time by looking at the clock but, by God, I knew many who had no education whatever!

In any event, a friend of this man's came to visit him. He had come from Cork, and had a fine watch. All present were staring at the watch, comparing it with the clock. It was put on a hook on the dresser so that they all could see it. Seeing it there, the man of the house stopped the clock. He was asked why he had done that. 'By God,' said he, 'isn't one of them enough, and wouldn't it be better to give the clock a rest while the watch is here?' He thought it might be good for the clock to be given a rest, lest it might get tired!

Here and there, before that, there had been sun-dials, but there were many who couldn't read these any more than they could the clock. The clock in those days was the cock, kept in the kitchen. He would be perched over the door or kept under the stairs, and he would be sure to crow at daybreak. That was the hour when the pookas and the sprites would be moving off, and then, from then on people could safely go off to a fair or to a market. It was said that it wouldn't be right to go out any earlier.

The cock, you see, had a power that no clock had; he could put the pookas to flight. Inside, over the door, the cock was usually kept, and he was able to keep out all evil. However, unless he was a March cock he would not be worth having at all. A black March cock is really the right cock.

I often saw one of them in a house and many is the time they tormented me by not allowing me to sleep very much of the night. If a cock were young he might crow even in the middle of the night. Should you be sleeping in the room with the cock in the kitchen, he could frighten the life out of you when he crew, and it could well happen then that you could sleep no more that night. Often I said to myself that I would chop off his head should I get the chance, whatever about the pookas.

All that must have been utter nonsense for, for a long time past, there is neither cock nor hen being kept inside in any house, and I don't hear of any harm being done by either the pookas or the sprites. They now have got a house to themselves, and it is better that way; they were filthy.

4. Schools and Schooling

I knew a Poor Scholar named Kingston. He had a school at the top of Coolnoohill (in the eastern extremity of the parish of Kilgarvan). It was a hedge-school he had there – a house of sorts with a thatched roof, built in a hollow. In it was a flagstone seat with a scraw laid on it. On that the pupils sat.

It is now forty years since Kingston taught there. The reason for it being there was that there was no other school nearer than Coolea and Morley's Bridge. Both were five miles away, and the journey would have been too long for the pupils.

A new school had been built at Morley's Bridge. That would have been quite convenient for the locals; otherwise they would have to go without schooling. £30 a year, I think, was what the master there was paid; his job was a poor one.

There was a man there named Michael O'Donoghue. When the new school at Morley's Bridge was built he could have got to being a master there, but he didn't take it. His livelihood was only the grass of three cows, and his holding was only a bit of wild mountainside. Presumably he preferred being able to take his ease. Later he regretted not having taken the job, but schoolmasters at the time were held in poor regard. There was no regard for anything but land, but a lot of the land was bad. Many had only the grass of a couple of cows. They would have goats too.

This hedge-school – Kingston's – was in Glanlea. A lot of people, with young families, lived there at the time. It was the farmers who built the house, and it was they, too, who paid Kingston; there was no one else to pay him at the time. Sixpence a week each pupil paid for the schooling.

There were over twenty pupils attending, and they would have no fire in winter; there was no fire-place. Slates they had for writing on, which they would place on their knees, but they learned no writing – only figures. I don't think there were any of them who could write, but they could read. I knew some of those, and there were many of them who couldn't make up figures. Some of those attending school there were up to twenty years of age. These would attend in the winter-time, but not during the summer as they would then have work to do at home, so that whatever they picked up one winter would have been forgotten when the next winter came. That was the situation in which they found themselves.

I knew an O'Donoghue boy who was very clever. He was an only child, and his people had the grass of three cows. When the Morley's Bridge school had been built the parish priest was prepared to appoint him there as a schoolmaster, but he refused the offer. He preferred to stay at home even though their farm was a poor one. That goes to show how senseless people then were.

At that time schoolmasters were being paid only £40 a year, but £40 was a lot of money in those days. It was better than three times as much today. Later schoolmasters' pay was raised to £60 a year, and then to £80. That was a lot of money in olden times – a quarry of money. And, look here, they are now being paid hundreds.

Every boy going to school would have a slate and a pencil. The pencils too, I think, were of slate. Kingston, when he had the school, would bring along the pencils and the pupils would buy them from him – a pencil and a slate each – for a penny. Each one's name was inscribed on his slate so that each would know his own.

Kingston knew both Irish and English, but he taught no Irish in the school. It was English he always spoke, although the people at that time had very little English – only trying to pick it up.

To punish pupils who didn't know their lessons Kingston had in the school an old horse-skull. Anyone not knowing a lesson would have to take the horse-skull home with him in the evening and bring it back next morning. He never beat anyone. He kept no rod, but most of the pupils, I think, would have preferred being beaten and get the matter over, rather than having to take home the old skull and having people making fun of them.

By Jove, you have got a horse-head today! In fact, even the horse had got a better head than yours![4]

There was a horse-skull in another school too. It was a man named Jeremiah O'Sullivan who taught there. In that school, too, the pupils had to take home the horse-head when they didn't know their lessons. He happened to have a bad pupil, and he gave him the horse-skull. The gorsoon took it, but when he got home he broke it with an axe. The Master composed a song about the affair – 'that he smashed my fine princely horse,' he said.

At Athnanoss, between the parishes of Glenflesk and Kilgarvan, there was another hedge-school. It was situated on the boundary. There was also one at Mangerton and another in Gortnaskeagh, in the parish of Kilgarvan, adjacent to Borlin.

Here at Athawn (near the Pass of Keimaneigh) there was another. Master O'Regan taught there, and he was a great teacher. Old people here remembered his being there; some of them had gone to school to him. There was no state school in Keimaneigh at the time, but there was one in Ballingeary.[5] That would have been four miles from Keimaneigh. Gougane is four and a quarter miles from Ballingeary.

The farmers built a school where Denis O'Sullivan, the teacher now in Keimaneigh, has his house. That is at Athawn. A state school was built there later,[6] and Owen O'Sullivan,[7] Denis' father, taught there. That school continued there for a long time. Then, about thirty-two years ago, a new school was built up on the hill – on Carrigavranir. That now is Keimaneigh school. It is on the hill, in from the road.

Master O'Regan, who taught down at Athawn, had great Irish. He taught Irish – how to read and write it. Everyone here, at the time, knew Irish and had very little English. Before the establishment of the Irish college in Ballingeary there were only two people hereabouts who could read and write Irish – Mícheál Ó Suibhne of Gortafluddig and Seámus Ó Muimhneacháin of Gearnapeaka. They are both still alive, and now over eighty years of age. They attended Master O'Regan's school at Athawn, and it was from him they learned how to read and write Irish.[8]

Master O'Regan lodged locally in the houses – a night here and a night there. That's how they all managed. They went home in the evening with one of the pupils, and might often stay a week in the one house. They had to pay nothing as they taught the pupils of the house at night. There would have been three or four children, or more, in each house. In those days people would have three meals of potatoes but sometimes, maybe, they would have stirabout at night.

From Bantry, I think, Master O'Regan came. He was by far the best of the Poor Scholars of his time – very well educated and a great teacher. He had a great collection of books, and these he would read aloud for people assembled at the fireside at night. He knew the Fianna tales and many others as well. Each night the house would be full of people who had come to listen to him, anxious to pick up those tales which he had. In that way they themselves would come to know those tales and then tell them at wakes.

The vagrant schoolmasters were called Poor Scholars. They would stay a while here and a while there. There was one named Tomás Gaine – a Poor Scholar from Kerry. He had a farm in Lomaunagh, near Kenmare. He spent a while in Clydagh (at the foot of the Paps mountain in Kerry), and he taught there. However, when Clydagh got drowned[9] he had moved east to Toone's Bridge (east of Inchigeela in the parish of Iveleary), and he spent a while teaching there.

They were called Poor Scholars because they were really poor. They had to depend on the payments made by their pupils, which was very little. No one paid more than sixpence a week, and often not even that much. Excepting the odd one, like Tomás Gaine, they had no house of their own; he had a farm. Many of them had nothing at all, no more than the beggar-man.

The Poor Scholars travelled a great deal, setting up school here and there. They would each have only one school in any place, but they kept constantly on the move.

Proud, well off farmers, with a lot of land – kernaghs as they were called – would each have a private teacher to teach their families. These teachers were kept in the house, paid so much a week, and fed. That's how things were before the establishment of the state schools. The poor people and the small farmers, however, had to depend on the hedge-schools, and there were many who never went to school.

It is seventy years since I first went to school. There was then a state school in Kilgarvan where Felim Cronin was the headmaster. Previously he had been a Poor Scholar, and I think the new school had been only fifteen years in Kilgarvan before I went to school there. The state schools had not been long at all in existence at the time. Daniel O'Connell had been responsible for them being introduced, but the hedge-schools continued for a long time afterwards in places. Then when the state schools came into being the Poor Scholars were recognised as masters, at least those of them deemed to be suitable.

This school in Kilgarvan looked quite new. The girls' school was over ours, on a loft. Thus it was a dual school. On one side was a door into ours, and another into the girls' school, with stairs leading up to it. In that a lady taught the girls. Her name was Annie O'Donovan. She married Geoffrey Curran, a shop assistant.

Each day, from the first of November to the beginning of April, we each brought two sods of turf to school. Anyone who failed to bring the two sods would get the stick and would not be allowed to go near the fire, whether feeling cold or not. Anyhow, no one would feel the cold after being flogged with a stick. That in itself was like fire!

At the time there were sixty boys attending the school, and approximately the same number of girls. Some of the pupils travelled up to six miles to school. We had, in all, four masters: Felim Cronin, the headmaster, two sons of his – James and Felim – and Batt Gill, another.

For doing sums I had a slate, but I had a copybook for writing. We had to pay a penny for that. I also had a pen and ink, but I had no pencil. The master had a blackboard and chalk. Each year we had to pay tuppence for the ink and a penny for the pen. We had also to pay for a map – a large map – hung on the wall. Each pupil had to have threepence to pay for that.

On Saturdays, except while we were learning the Catechism, we would have no school. For a month or two before the coming of the Bishop we would spend part of each Saturday in the school and another while in the chapel. Some would be learning the Catechism in Irish – the priest's clerk teaching them. They were those who had got no education, having never been to school. Some of them were twenty years of age when coming to the chapel to learn the Catechism. They were hard to teach, nor, indeed, did they learn very much either.

I remember a woman who was attending when I, myself, was being prepared for Confirmation. She was married to a man named Harrington. At this time she was sixty-five years of age and had her family reared. It was not until then that this woman was Confirmed. And she was not the only woman who had never been to school; there were many others as well. These could neither read nor write, and they probably only barely knew their prayers. Those people, at that time, were not required to know very much for Confirmation, as they had little or no education. Had it been made too difficult for them they could never get Confirmed, so things were not made too hard for them.

I, when going to school, knew both Irish and English, but my Irish was far better than my English. I learned the Catechism both in Irish and English. I was in the third book when I learned it, 'God save the mark!', as Jerry Coakley used to say.

The master taught no Catechism in Irish at school. It was all English. Every effort was being made at the time to suppress Irish. Anyone who might speak even one word of Irish at school would get flogged with the stick, and many of those attending were really to be pitied for their language was exclusively Irish, knowing only the odd word of English, just like their people at home. A leathering with the stick was the punishment, as far as I can recall. I saw no tally-stick being used, nor did I ever hear of it except the tally-stick being used by farmers and their servant boys. All the masters were very hard on pupils who spoke Irish; they considered only themselves, being afraid, as they were, of the Inspectors who visited the schools.

I knew the ABC before ever I went to school. I had already learned that. We had got to know it at home, in a sort of verse in Irish, but I have now almost forgotten it.

A: big mouth, it eats a potato.
C: the horseshoe.
D: a shoe heel.
F: the cat's whiskers.
G: the goblin.
J: the hurley.
K: the key.

That's all I now remember of it, but that's how I first learned the ABC. That's the way the old people had it, and it was from them I got it.[10]

I knew many who had never spent a day at school. It was a queer life. Early on there were no schools, nor was there any mention of education. People at that time didn't like paying out very much wages. When the eldest of a family grew to boyhood schooling for him was never even alluded to; the only thought was to send him out working and earning.

In Knockaruddig (in the parish of Kilgarvan) there was a man known as Tuaim Dearg. He was one of the Twomeys. He had never spent a day at school and was unable to read or to write, nor could he calculate figures. It was said, nevertheless, that he had money in the bank.

One day the priest was holding a station in the house of a man of the Sweeneys. He was chatting. 'Why,' said he to the man of the house, 'don't you send your children to school?'

'Well,' he replied, 'I can't see what good that would do.'

'An educated man can earn a good living,' said the priest.

'I'm not aware that it is so,' said Mr Sweeney. 'There's Mike O'Leary who is well educated, and, should you need a pound, had you better go to him or to Tuaim Dearg of Knockaruddig?'

Mike O'Leary was very well educated, but he had no money. The priest was left dumbfounded, nor did he say anything. That's the way things were at the time; people considered learning and schooling to be utter folly and waste of time.

You might, of course, say that no one could successfully manage without being educated, but there were people who did. I never saw any of them who failed. People took cattle and calves and pigs and sheep to the fair. They sold and they bought, and I never saw them being mistaken in any bargain they made. That often surprised me. They all were able to count money, and even able to mark sheep on the mountain with tar so as to be able to identify them. That they did, and so they were able to recognise their own from any strange sheep that might get mixed up with their own.

Tadhg Sweeney lived in Knockaunavona (in the parish of Kilgarvan). He had no education; he had never spent a day at school. Now, I saw that man marking his sheep with tar – putting TS as nice as ever you have seen on the side of each sheep. My father also did likewise, and he had no education; he would put PB on his sheep with tar. There were many like that, and they managed.

That was all right, but how did they manage when it came to counting money – those people who couldn't read a word and didn't know even the ABC. Should the money be notes they were able to identify the £10 note. On that would be TEN – three letters – and that's how they recognised it. Then the £5 note: that would have FIVE on it – four letters. And the £3 note: on that would be THREE – five letters. On the £1 note, too, there would be three letters – ONE – but no one could fail to observe that that was quite different to the £10 note.

Then regarding the change. They were all able to recognise a half-crown, a two-shilling piece and a shilling; they had no difficulty with these. To distinguish between coppers and silver they had only to look at the coins.

In those days, too, there were tenpenny bits, but they are now completely gone.

> My heart's darling was the tenpenny bit
> For off my heart it would take the thirst.

It was a silver coin, smaller than a shilling. There was also the shilling, the sixpence, the threepenny bit, and the fourpenny piece. The fourpenny piece was silver too. There were no tenpenny bits around in my time, but I did see them when I was young. They have gone out for the past eighty years. There was no need for them.

The half-sovereign was nicknamed the grasshopper. It was a gold coin. They were quite numerous in olden times, and so were the sovereigns. They have both long since disappeared. There was also the guinea – twenty-one shillings – but guineas are no longer mentioned except at auctions. The guinea was slightly larger than a sovereign.

There was also, in olden times, the crown-piece, but that, too, has long since disappeared. It was quite big. There was also the four-shilling piece, but that also got knocked out.

I have never seen a *cianóg* – a mite – but I did often hear it mentioned. Its value was half a farthing and so, indeed, it wasn't worth much. Often a person might say of something: 'It wasn't worth a mite', meaning that it was worthless. Even the farthings have gone, although, at one time, they were quite plentiful. One could then have bought a thing for a farthing, but now it would earn nothing better than abuse!

I have seen uneducated people counting cattle in their own way. Those with stock would recognise each animal by its unique markings. One might be white-faced and another white-loined, say with a white streak on its back, or it might have two white legs. These markings were noted, and indeed they had to be by those who couldn't count. In that way they could discover when a beast happened to be missing. One might be heard to say: 'I fail to see the white-loined. I'll have to search for her lest she might have fallen into a hole.'

A gorsoon unable to count might be sent out to look for the cattle. He would be wearing a cap, and he would take it off and collect pebbles. He would then put into the cap a pebble for each animal he could see and take those along home. At home there would be someone able to count. Should the stock, however, be not too large, he might then, perhaps, count those he could see on his fingers – a finger for each animal – and in that way his count would be entirely correct.

5. Saint Finbarr and Gougane Barra

Saint Finbarr started at Tobar na Naomh (i.e., The Well of the Saints) in Glenflesk (in Kerry). He had come there, I think, from Tipperary. Tobar na Naomh is a little bit in from the road in Glenflesk. The townland is called Droumavraka, and the land on which is the well is owned by Patrick O'Donoghue. A short round is paid at the well, and people come there for that on 8 May, I think.

The well is small, but the water in it is good. It is at the foot of a hill. There was neither a house nor a chapel there. The round is performed right around it to a corner in the west, and there is a sort of ledge on which to walk. Water would lodge on the ground in wet weather. The ledge, you might say, is two feet over the ground level.

Anyhow, St Finbarr left Tobar na Naomh and came to Gougane. He set out up to Foileeyerlaha (between Glenflesk and Kilgarvan). There is a path there still. He reached Inchees and then went up through Gortlahard and Coomnamein and Knockanuha (all in the parish of Kilgarvan), and then down into Eskwee (on the mountainside overlooking Gougane Barra).

At the corner of Gougane Island, on the way in, there are flagstones. These were there even then. St Finbarr came in that way to the island but, by oversight, he had left his spectacles behind him at Tobar na Naomh. Their mark is still to be seen on the well-slab.

St Finbarr having announced that he had forgotten his spectacles, word was passed from mouth to mouth all the way back. None moved a step, but the spectacles were passed back from hand to hand all the way from Tobar na Naomh to Gougane. Wasn't that extraordinary? It must have been St Finbarr's own attendants, who had been following him, who did it. Anyhow, having reached Gougane, he lived there for three years.

St Finbarr had a boatman named Loinín. It was from him that the Lee got its name, and I'll tell you how. He was bringing a sack of turf in to the island, on the western side of the lake. His boat got overturned, and he was thrown into the water. In the lake there was a monster. He snapped him up and swallowed him.

People saw this happen. They shouted that Loinín was drowned. They ran, they got staves and went searching. They drove the monster east down the river, prodding in and out with the staves. One would say: 'He is leeing (i.e., lying) there', and so on. They got down as far as Easach Loinín (Loinín's Waterfall) in the townland of Gearnapeaka. Over the waterfall the monster tumbled, but, having fallen, he belched up Loinín safe and sound, and he lived for years afterwards. From the crowd having been shouting 'He is leeing here' and 'He is leeing there' did the river get named the Lee.

Later when St Finbarr left the place he took Loinín with him. He had him as a servant.

At that time, and for long afterwards, Gougane, and up as far as Coomroe, was cluttered up with trees. I don't know who named the place Gougane, but the correct name of the townland is Dirreenacosha, and, by right, Keimaneigh is Dirreendonea. No one now calls it anything but Keimaneigh, and everyone refers to Dirreenacosha as Gougane. Now there are no trees worth mentioning there.[11] I have heard it said that Gougane means a place enclosed by rocks and with only one entrance to it. That could be right; that's exactly how it is.

I have also heard others say that there was no passage-way into the island until St Finbarr came there. It is said that it was St Finbarr who made the roadway into it. That, too, could well be correct, for anyone standing there, and looking at the place, would come to the conclusion that a roadway had been built there. Only a couple of yards of water had to be filled in. It would have been easy to build the roadway.

It is also said that no water was flowing out of the lake until then. St Finbarr and his followers arrived and set about making the roadway. I presume St Finbarr had by then decided to stay there.

Anyhow, Loinín, one of St Finbarr's followers, fell into the lake. There was a monster who swallowed Loinín. Then St Finbarr banished the monster from the lake. He headed eastwards, and the crowd followed him. In his efforts to escape the monster cut through the ground a passage or a track. He reached the top of Gearnapeaka, with the water following him through the track which he had cut. Looking now at the eastward course of the river one would have to agree that it would be hard to find anything more crooked. Eventually the monster got as far as large rock, and over that he tumbled and belched Loinín out on the ground safe and sound. The water then rolled down over the rock, and that waterfall is still called Easach Loinín (i.e. Loinín's Waterfall).

That could hardly be true, but so the story goes; and it has also been said that St Finbarr followed the monster down as far as Cobh and drove it into the sea there.

It must have been to Cork that St Finbarr went when he left Gougane. Cork city is divided into two halves which lie east and west of St Patrick's Bridge. There the river divided the city. The place was but a kind of a marsh in olden times.

And now, this is how Cork got its name. There there was a man named Corc Ó Doinn. He had built part of the city – the eastern half. West of the river there was another tribe, and he and they quarrelled. They wanted to prevent him from going ahead with what he was doing. There were starlings in the place, and it was about the end of November. They joined with Corc Ó Doinn in the fight, for the place had been kind to them. He then sent for St Finbarr to come and work out an agreement, and that's what first brought St Finbarr to Cork. And it was from Corc Ó Doinn that Cork was named.

It is also said that St Finbarr got himself a vantage point in Inchamore (about half a mile east of Keimaneigh) in the hope that from there he might see Cork. That point is upon the hill-side, but Cork wouldn't be visible from it.

The top of Inchamore is known at Cloch Bharra (i.e., Finbarr's Stone). There flagstones lie one over the other with a sort of cave underneath, in Mike Callaghan's farm-yard – just outside the dwelling-house door. Mike now uses it as a car-house. It is said that it was St Finbarr who set it up. In any event, the signs are still there.[12] I have never heard what he wanted it for.

Cloch Bharra lies about a mile and a half south-east of Gougane, as the crow flies. The distance would be more should one take the road.

I have heard it said that St Finbarr spent only three years in Gougane. There he lived on the island. He must have had some sort of a residence there but, however, there is no trace of it now.

On the island a cross stands between the cells, or arches, and there is something resembling a tomb at the foot of that cross. It is there St Finbarr's cell was, but all that remains now is a mound or little ridge. A tomb, I imagine, must have been there. It is to the north of it that Father Hurley is buried.[13] Long ago, when the Firbolgs were in Ireland they used to make extremely big and wide graves, and all who died would be buried in one of these, all together. What's now where the cross stands looks very like one of those.

The arches were built so that people could pray inside them; often, when the round was being paid the day might be wet. There are eight of these cells, in the enclosure on the island, and another by the roadside outside where Father O'Mahony's tomb stands.

Where Father O'Mahony came from I can't say, but he was never a parish priest here. On the island he had a little house where he lived until he died. He was there when Cromwell's soldiers came to Ireland. Hunting for him they went in to the island. He was there, but they failed to find him. I don't know how he lived while there, nor have I heard of anyone being with him. It was he, perhaps, who built the old chapel which was on the island. He is buried where the first arch, by the roadside, stands. It was Father Hurley who got the tomb built and an iron gate erected outside it.

The Stations of the Cross were put up on the island when the first High Mass was celebrated there. That would have been on 29 September, fifty-nine years ago last September. You could make the Stations of the Cross there, but that has nothing to do with the round. Before that the Stations hadn't been there.

At that time Father Hurley was parish priest here, and it was he who put up the Stations. It was he, too, who was responsible for High Mass being celebrated on the island. Also it was he who, beforehand, had built the new chapel. He was a good priest and did great work here. He also had intended building a monastery at Carrigadrohid, west of Gougane.

For the building of the chapel he collected money everywhere, but he did not seek any from the parish. Some came from America. Some of the parishioners also contributed, but there were others who, if anything, were opposed to what he had planned. However, had it not been for Father Hurley it is doubtful if High Mass would ever have been celebrated on the island, nor would the chapel have been built there. He was very devoted to Gougane and to the round, and he is buried on the island, beside St Finbarr's Cross – directly north of it.

When paying the round you would start outside at Father O'Mahony's tomb. There you would say five Our Fathers, five Hail Marys and five Glories. You would then go into the island and up to the cross. There you would repeat the same prayers. Then you would go to the first arch – the one on the left hand side on the way in. There you would double the prayers – this time saying ten Our Fathers, ten Hail Marys and ten Glories – and moving from arch to arch you would increase by five the prayers at each one of them, so that on reaching the eighth arch you would say forty Our Fathers, forty Hail Marys and forty Glories. From there you would go to where the old chapel altar was. There you could say any prayers you liked; there are no prescribed prayers.

On the way out you would wash in the well at the gate and pray there again, saying whatever prayers you liked.

Then you would go to the Slánán – a stream by the roadway outside; it is not on the island. You would drink a sup of the stream water, which is pure spring water. The water in the well shouldn't be drunk at all; you would only wash yourself with that. Again at the Slánán you would say five Our Fathers, five Hail Marys and five Glories, and then take a sup of the water. That would have completed the round.

The round at Gougane, I would say, is the longest paid anywhere, and it entails the saying of such a great number of prayers.

The Slánán never goes dry. It is pure spring water and rises on the hill above. That, it is said, is the water which St Finbarr used while he was in Gougane, and that's why it was named the Slánán – the Healer. Neither does the well go dry. It often falls very low in summer, but it fills up again when the rain comes. I have never seen it completely dried up. People drink the Slánán water; it is lovely water to drink. Often I have seen that water being sent to people down the country. People feeling unwell would send for it, and often it has cured them.

A person feeling unwell might promise to come to Gougane and pay the round there. Then, should he improve, he would come and do what he had promised. Very many did that. A person suffering from skin rash, or anything like that, would come and wash in the well, and that might cure him.

The round, in former times, was very popular. Many who were cured left their crutches behind them. Nothing like that happens now, but there are still people who feel they have been favoured by the round. I have heard people who have come say that they would come again.

There are still left traces of the old church. All who go to pray there, or many of them at least, leave behind them a token – a bit of cloth or match or a button or something else, even money; pence and halfpence were left. The old altar-stone is still there, and it is on that things were laid.

The old church was situated north of where the new one now stands. The altar-stone is all that is now left. To the east of it is a door-arch, and that's where Father O'Mahony had his house. There is no other trace now left.

I don't know when people first started coming to Gougane, but I have heard old people say that a child was born near Foiladav, between Rossalougha and Coomroe, who had seven noses. He used to come to Gougane every year and pay the round there, or maybe someone of his family would. Each year one of his noses would fall off. He kept coming for six years, but he didn't come the seventh year, lest he might be left without any nose at all!

Then, long ago, there happened to be a girl in Keimaneigh who was insane. She came to Gougane and went into the church – the new church. There she hid behind the altar. The man who was looking after the place closed and locked the door in the evening. He wasn't aware of anyone being inside. However, her people came searching for her. They found her in the church and took her home. However, there were people who said it was a pity they had not left her where she was, so that she would have got cured.

There was a woman who used to pay rounds in Gougane for payment. She often sent people a bottle of water which was said to have cured them but, then, anything which a sick person might long for and get would do him good.

This woman would pay the round for a shilling. She is now seventeen years dead. Often she sent a bottle of water to people in Limerick and Tipperary. She herself was from Tipperary, and her name was Ellen Burke. When she died she was buried in Gougane. This same woman would go to Ballyvourney for Whit Sunday and pay the rounds there, and also to Cathair Chrobh Dhearg near Rathmore (in Kerry). After Whit she would return and stay here until early November.

There is no one like her paying rounds here now. Another woman – a Mrs O'Neill – came, but the parish priest drove her away.

The first visit here is made on St John's Day and the previous night. Many came that night, and they still come. They would spend the night on the island; those in poor health would come and spend the night on the island. Then, they would pay the round.

The round could be paid at any time of the year, but that is usually done from 24 June up to the autumn. The round time extends up to the last Sunday in September. People came on that day and the previous night. That is known as Mass Sunday. High Mass is celebrated and a sermon is preached on St Finbarr.

Enormous crowds come on that Sunday – much larger than at any other time of the year. Four thousand and more have often come. They come from all quarters. Many came from Cork, and still do. I have got to know people who had come from various places, even many from overseas. They would call in to me here; the road passes by the door.

Each party coming would have their own particular night. Those from Kerry came over the hills on the last Saturday in August. That was known as the Kerry Saturday.

Others, too, had a special night – those from Inchigeela and Dunmanway and Kealkil. A couple of hundred would come from each parish. The Ballyvourney folk, too, had their own special Saturday. All others usually came earlier in the year than did those from Kerry. Then some might say: 'We'll wait for the Kerrymen'. They would have previously got to know them.

Those who came on a Saturday evening would spend the night up – drinking and singing and dancing. Still they would pay a round that night and another in the morning. They needn't have been fasting.

A few also came from Skibbereen. Vast crowds came from Cork City and stayed on for a couple of days. Indeed, many people came in the month of June, but most preferred the autumn when the feast of St Finbarr falls.

I have even seen people come from Sneem and Cahirdaniel (in Kerry). There has been no falling off in the crowds who come – up to the present at any rate. It is now fifty-five years since I myself started coming. We came every year from Lounihan. The journey would take only two hours across the mountain, and that at your dead ease. Over the mountain, walking, most people came in those days, but old people came by horse and cart, and some would come on horseback.

At that time there was no road leading to Gougane, only a path. Down at Keimaneigh cross there is a field. That was named Páirc na gCapall (The Horses' Field), and it still is. In there people put their horses and let them graze there for the night. It was owned by Mr Burke; the Burkes had always been there. It was there Máire Bhuí Ní Laoghaire – the poet – lived, she being married to the elder Elic Burke. Sixpence, or some small amount, was paid for the horses; Mr Burke wouldn't be hard on anyone. Unlike today, people then were in no way greedy. Those going now are mean and stingy; mehegawns Jerry Coakley would have called them.

Up from Keimaneigh cross, as far as Céim Got, south of the house here, there was a path. A man named Got is reputed to have killed a man there one morning as he was on his way back from Gougane. Who Got was I have never found out, nor do I know who it was that he killed. Anyhow, ever since the spot has been known as Céim Got.

An old path leads that way west to Gougane. Its traces are still there, south of the road. It was those coming to pay the round who made that pathway, throwing stones under their feet on the bog. Many of those stones are still to be seen there, but now that there is a road, no one uses the path.

On St John's Day and the previous night crowds came here. On one occasion a quarrel occurred between those from Iveleary and those who had come from Bonane (in the parish of Kilgarvan) and they walloped each other. The parish priest then prohibited the people here from coming to Gougane on St John's Day, or on the previous night, to prevent further quarrelling between themselves and those coming from Kerry. Never since have the people here come to Gougane on St John's Day; they wait until the autumn.

In former days they drank and they fought, and they and the Bonane crowd hurt one another. Some of those who had come from Kerry were so badly maimed that they remained over for a full week. Those coming in those days wanted only to fight – to be able to boast that one was better than the other. That was utter nonsense, and I have often told them so. They would boast to me that they had bested so and so, but I would say to them: 'I wouldn't fight without getting paid for it.' One would like to get paid for anything he did. No fear that you would now get anyone to do otherwise.

East of Father O'Mahony's tomb, up on a little hill, there is a graveyard. It has been there for a long long time. It was small at first, but a piece has been added to it. The only people originally being buried there, as far as I know, were the Callaghans of Rossalougha and the O'Learys of Geartha. I know of no others of the old stock who were buried there, but several others, too, later on in former times, came to be buried there. The place got filled up. A new section was added, and then people acquired graves there from the parish priest. Their families are now being buried there.

Before the new piece was added there would not have been room for more than a hundred graves at the most. The Cronins from Ballingeary then came to be buried there, and many other local people as well. Many also took graves in Inchigeela; there is a new graveyard to the east there. However, many of these have been reverting to Gougane. It is in Gougane that I myself will be buried, even though I have a place in Ballyvourney.

6. Old-Time Tailoring

Long ago Adam was a tailor in the Garden of Eden. He was stripped of his clothes when he sinned. He then made himself clothes of leaf tufts. He was the first tailor ever. There have been tailors ever since.

The tailor is the seventeenth part of a man, and I'll tell you how that came about.

A tailor who was in a certain street drank himself out. With nothing left he then started roasting potatoes and selling them to people who might call in. Seventeen tailors came in to eat them, and they each gave him a half-crown. Having got that money he resumed his tailoring, and eventually earned a lot. He then put up a plate on the outside of his window, and on it he wrote: 'Seventeen tailors made a man of me.'

Had it not been for the money which he got from them he would have been ruined, so that's what the saying means.

A scissors, a measuring-tape and a thimble, thread and an iron and chalk: these, at the time, were the tailors' tools. They had neither a machine nor anything else but these.

The back, the sides and the front, the skirt and the collar: these, as cut, make a coat, but there are also the sleeves. The skirt, or skirt coat, would have a slit in the back.

Before that there was the frock coat, called the swallow-tail. Indeed I made many of these too. I wouldn't mind which I had to make; they were nearly all the same.

Then, there were knee-breeches and long trousers. I preferred making the trousers. Knee-breeches were hard to make; two pairs of trousers would have been easier to make. A kind of door had to be made in the front. That closed on both sides. It had to be made so that it would fall down when the sides were opened. The breeches knees were hard to make; they had to be made to measure, exactly. There are none of them nowadays; they have gone out. And the frock coat: that, too, has gone.

The cut was not at all difficult if one had been taught it. A certain number of tapes were required, and it was slow work. Each round needed twenty-four tapes to cover the width to be cut. That was known as graduated measuring. It could be managed without that, but then it would have been only hit or miss. It had to be accurate; otherwise the fitting would not be right. Previously there were patterns, and they were a help. They were really slow to work with; it was like a blind man trying to catch a hare.

When taking a person's measure there would have been no book in which to enter the measurements. The tailor would have a piece of chalk with which to enter the measurements on the wall, or on a seat. The amount of cloth to be cut would then be cut. All the chalk in those days was of only one colour – white. White flannel would be marked with a bit of partly burned willow-rod. That would leave a black mark.

People would also have bits of willow-rods on Easter Sunday. They, too, would be partly burned and used to make a cross on the coat-sleeve. Everyone did that, but why I don't know.

When I first took up the trade no one went to the tailor, as they do now; the tailor came to the houses. He would spend a night here and a night there.

Tailoring is easy now; there is every facility. There is thread, but in olden times the thread had to be made at home. The housewife would have a spindle and a potato when making thread. The wool had to be very finely spun for thread-making. The spindle, you might say, would be ten inches in length. The wool would be made into little flat rolls and these, then, would be spun into thread. My mother made thread that way, and I saw her do it before ever I saw anyone else do so. The tailor had no other thread but that. Tailors used to come to our house at home.

My mother was the first I ever saw making thread. She would have a spindle and a potato, but, at the time, I never really got to know anything about what was being done.

There is probably no one now left who could make thread that way. It died out as it was no longer necessary.

To make the thread smooth the tailors would draw it through beeswax. It could then be easily pulled through the cloth; it could be very easily done.

At that time there were very few instruments, and only that people were as ingenious as they were they could never have managed. They had a knack for doing everything.

The tailor would come to the house. He would be sent for when one needed to get a suit of clothes made. He might then also make suits for the whole household.

There were yellow gilts of some sort of metal – brass, maybe. These gilts would be put on the coat. For trousers there were white buttons, and small gilts for waistcoats.

The white buttons were made from some sort of horn. They were brittle. Some of them too, I would say, were made of wood. Often, too, buttons were made from furze rods. The rods would be chopped, notched in the centre with a knife, and then sewn on where the notch was. That would do fine.

Snout-rings for pigs were also made out of furze rods. Two little pieces of these rods would be got and a notch would be cut at the top and bottom of each of them. Then, with an awl, a hole was made through the pig's snout. That would make do for a double snout-ring which would stay permanently in position. There was no other sort to be had in olden times.

Tailors also made caps. I often made one; we always made our own. A cap was easy to make. Caps then came to be made in the factories, and it was no longer worth while making them as we did.

I never made a hat. Rural tailors never bothered making them, but it was tailors who made them in the factories.

There is a sort of a block on which to set the hat, just as would be done when making a boot.

To make boots the shoemaker came to the house, just like the tailor. They both worked the same way. The shoemaker would stay at a house until he got his job finished.

Goat-skin was used for shoe-making before the shoemakers turned to cow-hide leather. An old goat would be killed and skinned. The skin would be placed in a hole. Some water and quicklime and oak-bark would then be got, and it was with these that the goat-skin was cured. That was the tannery.

The shoemaker wouldn't come until the leather was ready. Shoes in those days were poorly shaped, I would say. Tanneries were later set up and then other leathers came to be used – cow-hides and horse-hides.

The shoemaker has now got his own house, and he no longer has to go here and there. And so, too, the tailor: he, too, has got his own house and has a great time.

7. *Some Tailor Anecdotes*

'The tailor, the piper and the goat – the airiest three on the globe.'
So it is said, and is probably true, too. The whole world knows
that the goat is airy. He is a devil. He is constantly causing
damage or up to some mischief. 'When a goat enters a church he
goes right up to the altar.' That is a proverb. Everyone has a
whack at the goat for he is always being accused of something.

The piper is airy. He never likes staying in the one place.
There is never a dance nor a fair nor a feis that he won't attend,
having his pipes – airy and light-hearted.

It was the same with the tailors. An airy lot they were too
who kept constantly on the move from place to place. They
would spend a week with me and another with you. Their only
concern was to get paid, and they were easily paid in olden times;
the people for whom they worked fed them.

Of course times have greatly changed since then. Now every
tailor has got a house of his own and couldn't be got to move out
to anyone. He has got to keep himself, and keep his house.

When an airy tailor, as most of them were, came to a house
he would be welcome twenty times over. He would have an
apprentice who would accompany him. Food, at the time, was
scarce – not as plentiful as it is now, nor could people afford it –
whatever dainties the people might have the tailor was sure to
get his share.

People always tried to keep in with the tailor as they depended
on him to make their clothes. Everyone liked to have a good suit
to wear – a respectable suit, but they were also anxious that too
much cloth would not be wasted. There would be a bale of frieze
for the tailor when he came, and two or three, or maybe four,
would need a suit. The tailor could hack and waste the cloth if
he so desired, so it was best to be in with him.

People in olden times were very sparing with cloth. It was
frieze they then had, and the first remark from the woman of the
house to the tailor when he came was to warn him not to waste
the frieze.

A tailor came to a certain house and the first greeting he got from the woman of the house was: 'Don't waste any of the frieze.'

'I'll make no waste,' said he; 'never fear.'

However, no matter how the cloth was cut little bits would drop out of the opening being made as the cloth was being cut; that would happen with the best of tailors. The woman, however, thought that it was due to bad tailoring. As she moved about she saw a bit of the frieze on the floor. She picked it up.

'Oh, Dan,' said she to the tailor, 'I would have considered a little clipping to have been too much.'

'Ah, by God, woman,' said he, 'of what significance is a little scrap compared to getting a man's bones properly covered?'

'Oh, I beg your pardon,' said she, 'that didn't at all occur to me.'

'Indeed,' said the tailor, 'if it didn't it will later on.'

There was another tailor who went to a house to make a suit, or a couple of suits, for the family. The woman of the house warned him not to waste the cloth – that it was scarce. 'Oh, never fear,' said the tailor.

Anyhow, he cut the cloth, and little clippings fell off as it was being cut. 'Oh, now, now!' said she, 'all the cloth is being wasted.' She picked up the clippings and gazed at them. The tailor said nothing.

So far so good. Tea-time came, and she made the tea. All sat down to the table. The mistress cut the cake but some of it fell in crumbs as it was being cut. Up jumped the tailor. 'Oh, now, now!' said he, 'what a waste of bread! There it is being lost in useless crumbs.' He picked up the crumbs and kept looking at them, just as the woman had been staring at the clippings. Of course, she realised that the allusion was to herself and the clippings. She never came to mention the frieze again after that.

When the tailor had come to a house the neighbours would congregate in there every night. It would be a great get-together with a house full of them seated around. Each would have a story to tell – one trying to outdo the other. Heroic tales would be told and, hold your tongue, you have never heard stories such as they would have, however it was that they could have remembered them. They couldn't be excelled. You would have thought the night too short had you been listening to them.

It wasn't heroic tales at all the tailor would have to tell but of his own affairs and adventures here and there, and I doubt if it was the truth he always had to relate. No one believes a word from anyone who is known to be a liar, and that is the reputation which some tailors had. Still people visited the house at night, to which he had come just to hear what he might have to relate, and they thoroughly enjoyed it all.

But let me be! What times these were! People in those days were airy: they made fun for each other, joking and passing the time.

It is extraordinary the way these times are no more. They were both good and bad. They were really bad in some way: food was scarce and money was scarce. One might spend a whole year working and in return have nothing saved. Had people then not been as light-hearted as they were they could hardly have survived at all. The people today could never survive through times as bad as they had.

A tailor had come to work in a certain house and the neighbours came along night-visiting. He was a tailor who had very ugly feet and, like all other tailors, he would take off his boots when going to work on the table. Sitting on his hunkers on the table, he had his legs crossed. One was sticking out. The woman of the house, anyhow, was walking around. She glanced at the tailor's foot. 'I'll bet,' said she, 'that that's the ugliest foot any of you has ever seen.' Addressing the neighbours she was – making fun. By dad, they all laughed and looked at the tailor. 'I'll bet,' said he, 'that there's an uglier foot than it in this house.'

The woman was furious on hearing that for her own feet were not at all good, and that was something that hadn't occurred to her until then. She immediately made a bet. What their bet was I don't know – a gallon of porter, maybe. The tailor stuck out the second foot – his own – which he had under his bottom. That was much uglier than the other. There and then he had won the bet.

In Ballyvourney there was a tailor. He was known as Táilliúir na Samhna (the November Tailor). His name, I think, was Dan Herlihy. I knew him well; we often had a drink together.

Táilliúir na Samhna was an airy man. He was outstandingly fluent, with an unbeatable gift of speech and of everything else, I declare. He never married; he lived with his mother. They had a thatched house in Ballymakeera. I have seen the house, but I was never inside it.

'Tailor, why don't you marry?' people used to say to him.

'Damn you,' he would say, 'haven't I got the woman my father had before me, and isn't she quite good enough for me?'

Táilliúir na Samhna had an apprentice who had come from Carriganymid (in the parish of Ballyvourney). He too, I think, was one of the Herlihys, but of that I wouldn't be sure. Anyhow, he was a poor apprentice. He served his time with the tailor, and when his time was up the tailor told him he didn't need him any more. He then went home.

The cut had come in at the time. To learn it one would have to spend six months or thereabouts working for a tailor who had got it. Previous to that they hadn't got it; they had only a pattern. With that the work was slow, but they managed. Táilliúir na Samhna hadn't got the cut, nor had any other tailors either at the time. In this country the tailors didn't have it. They had got it in England and in Scotland long before the tailors in Ireland had.

The apprentice's mother imagined that the Tailor had the cut, but she found out that her own boy hadn't learnt it. Post haste, by Jove, east she went to Táilliúir na Samhna.

'My boy,' said she, 'has spent his time here with you and, having served his time, isn't it strange that he has not got the cut?'

'Indeed, he has,' replied the tailor.

'I tell you he has not,' said she.

'Of course he has,' said he, 'but the cut he has is the bread-cut.'

The apprentice had a good appetite, but otherwise – for tailoring – he was useless.

Táilliúir na Samhna used to make uniforms for the peelers, and mend them – working in the barracks. The peelers had a servant-girl. Anyhow, one evening the Táilliúir heard the girl say that she would make a sweet cake. By Jove, he wasn't at all pleased that he himself wouldn't be there to get some of the cake to eat. He had been there a couple of days working at the time.

The girl put the cake to bake. The Tailor was still at work, and one of the peelers was in the room inside. The Tailor asked the girl to go over to the pub and get a half-gallon of porter for himself and the peeler. He was just finishing up and the girl had taken up the cake and left it to cool. She set off. The Tailor gathered up his tools, stowed the cake into his bag, and set off out the door. He went east home and ate the cake himself, leaving the girl and the peeler in the lurch over west!

I don't know why he was called Táilliúir na Samhna. There was some reason for it, but what it was I don't know. But there was another tailor in Coolea who was known as Táilliúir na Cásca (the Easter Tailor). He was in no way related to Táilliúir na Samhna. Táilliúir na Cásca, I think, was a Lynch, and they were both around at the same time – himself and Táilliúir na Samhna.

Táilliúir na Cásca got married, but he took himself off soon afterwards. To England he went, I think, and never returned. A few songs were composed about his going away, and I have heard them. His wife was known as Méin. Anyhow, a certain poet said:

> I'll fly off like a goose
> And go away a-roving
> Like Pascha did from Méin.

Pascha – Easter – he called the Tailor.

Táilliúir na Samhna had a dog. He had called that dog Friday. He went to work back to The Mills – making a suit for one of the Protestants who were there at the time. His dog was with him.

He happened to be there on a certain Friday and, of course, he wouldn't eat meat that day. The Protestants were poking fun at him about the meat, seeing that he wouldn't eat it. 'I'll bet,' said one of them, 'That your dog will eat meat.' They put meat on a plate in front of the dog. He moved towards it – to eat it, just like any dog would do. 'Friday! Friday! you devil,' said the Tailor to him. The dog stopped. He went towards it a second time, but the Tailor again spoke up: 'Friday! Friday! you devil. What do you think?' said he. The dog turned on his heel and went off.

The Tailor surprised all those present. It had never occurred to them that the dog's name was Friday.

Near Kilgarvan there was a tailor who had an apprentice. The apprentice's name was Dan Doyle. They worked in the houses. They happened, one morning, to be crossing a river. Dan was a small little man. There were steps across, and the master crossed over. The apprentice went to follow him, but he fell and was swept off by the flood. The master shouted, and the neighbours heard him. They came and set off in search of the apprentice. He was only barely able to swim, and when he surfaced he looked around him. He saw the neighbours on the bank. 'If you don't save me,' said he, 'the Laune people will soon be left without a tailor!'

Anyhow, somehow or other they saved him and took him to the house. He was drenched wet. He went to bed, and his clothes were put to dry. The woman of the house boiled a drop of milk for him; she said that it would do him good. 'Hold on a while,' said the old tailor. He cut a slice of bread and handed it to the woman. 'Give him this,' said he, 'and tell him that that is the cut!'

Tailor Crowley (Tadhg Crowley) and his family lived in Ballyvourney. He was the limit! He was a poet, and he had a great command of speech. He could compose a song about anything at all, and his family were equally gifted when they grew up.

His house was on the boundary dividing Dirreenauling from Derrynasaggart (townlands in the parish of Ballyvourney). He used to say that every night he took off his boots in Dirreenauling and went to bed in Derrynasaggart. The kitchen was on the Dirreenauling side of the boundary and the bedroom east in the Derrynasaggart side.

He was an extraordinary man, God rest his soul! Himself and his sons used to work together, and compose poetry; they were entirely unique. Some of the sons stayed at home, and one or two of them left: they went to England or to America. His son Pádraig is still alive. I knew him well – a fine man. He has grand Irish and he is a fine poet – every bit as good as his father.

There was a man in Coolea who was known as Diarmaid na Beárnan. His name was Diarmaid Lynch. No one, at the time, would be allowed to kill a hare. The landlord, I assure you, would not have permitted it, and anyone who might kill one would pay dearly for it. The landlord could have him evicted from his land, and no one could avenge it on him.

Anyhow, Diarmaid caught a hare, put it into a bag and took it off with him. He had intended complaining to the landlord that he was being tormented by the hares – eating all he had – but someone took the cord off the bag and set the hare free.

Tailor Crowley then composed a song about the hare, claiming that it was a cat which had gone astray and telling how he had sent off his brother everywhere in search of him:

In the bag there was much that I couldn't for you reckon
But there was in it a white-headed cat, as far as I know,
Who wouldn't leave a rat in a stack nor a mouse in a hovel,
And what a loss he has been to all here at home.

He then sent his brother searching for him:

In a dash he set off away south to Kinsale,
And returning he came through Moyratha.[14]
In the Oultig[15] he got afflicted and suffered great pain
And barely escaped drowning in the ford of Akahan.[16]

He searched everywhere, pretending to be looking for the cat.
Having found no trace of him he returned home and then, by
Jove, he said that where the cat was found was under the bed in
Billy Count's house, on a Sunday morning:

On a Sunday morning in Billy Count's house
He was heard under the bed miaowing.

Billy Count could in some way have well been involved. He used
to look after the land for the landlord, and should anyone
misbehave he would pay dearly for it; Billy Count would immediately report him.

Two tailors and two carpenters were working in a house east in
Inchanossig (midway between Keimaneigh and Ballingeary).
Anyhow, on a Friday, they were given potatoes and butter for
dinner. At the time the plate would be put in the middle of the
table so that each one could take a bit of the butter with his knife
and put it on the potato and eat it.
    The carpenters were better at eating the butter than were the
tailors. On the side of the butter which was facing them there
soon came to be a hollow. Only the four of themselves were
eating, and the woman of the house was attending to something.
'Ah, boys, why don't you eat the butter?' said one of carpenters,
and there and then he took the plate and turned the side which
was still intact towards himself.
    Later when the woman of the house came around she
thought it was the tailors who had eaten all the butter.

A tailor was working in a house where they had no meat. The

man of the house told his son to go out and kill a deer so that they would have it for dinner. Out he went, but he failed to kill any deer. It is only by chance that one could kill a deer: he is too fleet-footed, and he could scent anyone drawing near.

The son returned home. They had a black sheep, and the father then told him to kill it, which he did. They cooked some of it for the dinner. They then had both potatoes and meat for dinner, and they all sat to the table. The man of the house raised his head and spoke to his son: 'Yes, Tadhg,' said he, 'not having got the deer the black sheep will be good to eat.'

That would be said should you have got something as a substitute for something else.

Long ago there was a tailor in Bonane (south of Kenmare). By Jove, in a fit he crossed over the hills to Kealkil, and never stopped until he got to Dunmanway. He stayed there and went to work.

At the weekends he used to lodge in a certain house. Eventually he had £40 saved. He fell sick and he gave the £40 to the man of the house on condition that when he died he would be taken to St Fiachna's Cemetery for burial.[17]

Anyhow, this other man had the £40 when the tailor died. This was about three weeks before Christmas. They shouldered him over across and buried him in Inchigeela. Taking him there was much easier than taking him to Bonane.

Having buried him they walked out, and then the man who had got the money looked back, and said he: 'He has got from now until Christmas to get home to St Fiachna's.'

8. Spirits, Pookas and the Good People

Casadh na Spride (i.e., The Spirit Turn) is on the road east at Droumanallig. It is not fully a quarter of a mile west of Ballingeary. It is just east of Creedon's house, which is on the roadside. While I have known the spot it is reputed to have had pooka associations. There was a spirit there in former times.

A man named Michael Creedon lived in Illaunynagh. He fought a spirit there. She would appear in the form of a woman, and only those out late at night would see her. Late one night Michael was on his way home. The spirit accosted him on the road, just at the turn. She used to put a problem to people and would kill anyone who failed to solve it. I believe that she killed people there, but I don't know who these were.

'A candle and a candlestick there is, and you fit a couplet to that,' she would say. That is what she would say to those whom she met, as she had been condemned to stay there until someone solved her problem for her. She had done something wrong. Such were the spirits – after death.

Michael Creedon had no option but to respond to the couplet. Said he: 'Holly agrowing in a glen, and being put as a roof on a house.'

'That doesn't answer my question,' said she, and she repeated her couplet. She would allow one to make three efforts.

Michael tried again: 'A mill on a river mangling, and striking on all sides,' said he.

'That doesn't answer my question,' said she again. She then posed her problem for the third time, and then said Michael: 'You ought to have got to Heaven in time rather than being a ghost as you are!' He had no sooner said that than she disappeared up into the air. No one has ever since seen her.

On the way through Mangerton Mountain to Killarney there are six or seven burial-mounds. Under each of these a person had been buried, and it is said that all of these had been killed by a spirit. They look like grave headstones.

I would say that the death of those people was mostly due to cowardice – that they died of fright. People were terrified of these spirits in those days; they often killed people.

Below Morley's Bridge (in the parish of Kilgarvan) there was a man who was known as Amhlaoibhín Bán. He was one of the Lynches. He and Micil Bán, who had a shop in Macroom, were the sons of two brothers. Seán Morley lived near the bridge at the time, and I believe that it was from one of his people that Morley's Bridge got its name.

Anyhow, one Sunday Amhlaoibhín Bán was on his way home from Mass when he met Seán Morley. He asked Amhlaoibhín to come to him scythe-mowing next day – that he had work for two west on the hill. Amhlaoibhín arrived next morning, and they both set off west. That was in the month of August.

It was late, and night had fallen, when they got back to Morley's Bridge. They had their supper. Shortly afterwards Amhlaoibhín set off for home, with his scythe on his shoulder. Down near the school he met a neighbour who was on a saddle-horse. They spoke, and the neighbour said that his horse had only one shoe and that he was on his way to the forge.

They parted, and Amhlaoibhín continued on homewards. He thought that Diarmaid – the neighbour – would catch up with him on the way. He went on down to the crossroads. From there, there was a short-cut up to his own house. However, before he got in the spirit appeared in front of him, and wouldn't allow him in. That was the first time Amhlaoibhín had seen her, although it had been said that she was there.

He attacked her with the scythe. He was quite courageous as he thought that Diarmaid would come along any minute and that he would then have help. He thought he had split her in two, but she gave no indication of surrender. She escaped and gave three yells that could be heard in the Far East. She attacked him again, but Amhlaoibhín continued to defend himself. She tried to close in on him, but he kept warding her off with the scythe.

He jumped aside when she came to attack him for the second time. He then put his back to the fence to prevent her getting behind him. He kept his face to the road and backed up the field, but she didn't follow him. Backing all the while, he got in home and saw no more of her.

He went to bed, but next morning his left hand was so swollen that he could do nothing with it. He sent for the priest, who came and told him he needn't worry – that he would have nothing wrong with him; and he was right. The swelling left and there were no ill-effects.

That's how he escaped from the spirit. It was he himself I

heard relate it all, and indeed I won't belie him now. He said that he would hardly have succeeded only that he thought he would have heard Diarmaid coming along any minute; that kept up his courage.

That was one of the Mangerton spirits, but there were more than one. I have heard that there were many of them there.

I have heard that it was white-handled knife which would kill a spirit, if she were stabbed with that knife. I have heard too that there was a man who stabbed and killed a Mangerton spirit with a white-handled knife which he had. He had it in his pocket. He must have come prepared for her.

Many people had fought that spirit, but if they did she overcame them. 'Stab and pull' is what she used to say to them. That they should stab the knife in, and then pull it out again, was what she wanted.

One night, however, a man came along with the knife in his pocket. She jumped out at him, and he went to fight her. He took out the knife. 'Stab and pull, stab and pull,' she said. She jumped towards him, and then jumped away again. Then a voice spoke into his ear, 'Stab, but don't pull,' said the voice. Up to then he had been stabbing her with the knife and then pulling it out again. This time, however, he stabbed her with the knife and left it stuck in her. She immediately fell to the ground, lifeless. The man then ran off and went home. Next morning he came back and found the knife. There it was, stuck in something like frog-spawn. There was no other trace of the spirit; the knife had killed her. Had the voice not spoken into his ear it is he himself who would have been killed and not the spirit. She could have bided her time until he got exhausted, and then she would kill him.

I have heard it said that neither a spirit nor any other evil being was capable of crossing water – that is to say a river or stream. I don't know if that is true, but old people believed it was. I myself have never seen a spirit, thanks be to God!

I knew a man who had a son of school-going age. This now I have seen with my own eyes. The gorsoon misbehaved in some way, whatever it was, and his father chastised him, giving him a terrible beating. These people were Sweeneys. Having been thrashed as he was, the gorsoon went off to bed, but at some hour of the night he slipped out and there was no trace of him in the morning. They went searching for him but failed to get any tidings of him anywhere. His father thought he might have enlisted; there were soldiers in Tralee at the time.

On his saddle-horse the father set off and never stopped until he got to Tralee, but, by God, the gorsoon wasn't there. He turned for home, and it was well into the night when he was approaching Killarney. When he reached Cromagloun (in the parish of Kilgarvan) something so frightened his horse that he couldn't get him to go ahead. He himself saw nothing, but the horse stalled and refused to go past whatever was there. He then turned aside and took to a path. Even though he had seen nothing he was terrified. His horse was trembling and foaming white at the mouth.

Eventually he got home and stabled his horse. Then he went off to bed. Having got up next morning he went out to have a look at the horse. He was a big bay horse with a black mane and tail, but the horse's mane and tail were now grey. He came back in and told of what he had seen, and when the people of the house looked at himself his hair too was grey, even though it had previously been black. Neither himself nor his horse were otherwise affected, but they both remained grey ever afterwards.

Unknown to him the gorsoon had been down by the Laune. There he spent two years working for a farmer, and then he returned home.

People nowadays wouldn't believe in those things. Thank God, there is no longer anything like that, but it wasn't always so. Times have improved. Neither priest nor friars were then as numerous as they are now. In former times there was only one priest between Toone's Bridge (in the eastern extremity of the parish of Iveleary) and Coomroe (west of Gougane Barra). That's seventeen miles. Taken together, lengthwise and breadthwise, that's a big territory. Now there are three priests in the parish. When priests were not easily at hand many must have died without being given Extreme Unction. That must have been why they had to suffer Purgatory and that so many from the next life reappeared.

There are also the air-demons. These are devils who were banished from Heaven and who have been roaming the world ever since. These, it is said, would have done much more harm than they did were it not that they hoped to be allowed back into Heaven on the Last Day.

Long ago there was a spirit at Carrigafooka (in the parish of Kilnamartyra), on the road leading from Ballyvourney to Macroom. I haven't heard that she ever killed anyone, but she used to appear there.

In Coolea there was a man named Donncha Dinneen. He was nicknamed Donncha an Eireabaill (i.e., Donncha of the Tail), and this is how he got that nickname. An old man died who had a swallow-tail coat; that was the sort worn by old people. When he died Donncha was given that coat, and it was from that coat-tail that he got the nickname.

He was a young man and was planning to go to America. He had saved up £8. He said nothing. He went to bed one night, and then in the middle of the night he set out. There were no clocks in those days, so he didn't know what time it was. He set off towards Macroom, intending to slip away unknown to his family.

He set out – walking – east through Ballyvourney and on to Carrigafooka. There the spirit leaped out in front of him. He jumped away from her, moving backwards, but she followed him. However, she didn't attack him. In off the road a cock crew in a house, and when he did the spirit disappeared and he saw no more of her. However, he had got such a fright that he immediately set off back homewards. He didn't go to America at all, and were it not for the spirit he would have sneaked away.

Later on he married Máire Mhór. She was a big woman – one of the Creedons. Her mother was Neil Bheag (i.e., Little Nell) Sweeney. She married twice. Her second husband was Seán Meirgeach Mahony. He came from Kilmichael.

Over here in Keimaneigh there was a man of the Sweeneys who used to see the pookas. He was known as Diarmaid a' Chéama. He died a few years ago, and he was the last man here who used to see the pookas.

On one occasion he happened to be returning home from Cork, with his horse. At the time there was a woman over in Tooreenlehard. She was one of the Learys, and was married to a man of the Lehanes. It was well into the night when Diarmaid reached the top of Rossmore (east of Inchigeela). There he saw saddle-horses coming towards him on the road. It was the pookas who were there, and riding behind one of them, on a horse, was this woman. He caught her by the leg and dragged her off the horse, just as they were going past him. He took her home. The pookas didn't follow them at all.

That woman lived for many years afterwards. Had Diarmaid
not snatched her off with him she would have been dead in the
morning. Nothing happened to her.

It has been said that the pookas couldn't take away anyone
without having someone from this world with them. There
must have been someone with them that night; Diarmaid
wasn't with them at all.

There was a man in Kilgarvan. His name was Seán O'Connor. He
too used to be out with the pookas. Old Seán Sweeney lived in
Steelaghs (in Borlin, but in the parish of Kilgarvan). He had a
daughter named Máire. She, by God, was struck down sick and
had her people distressed and tormented. She was neither getting better nor any worse. Her father, Seán, eventually went to
Seán O'Connor, who was reputed to be going out with the
pookas. There was nothing going on that he didn't know.

The girl's father had come to the conclusion that it wasn't at
all their own daughter whom they had – that the pookas had
taken her off and replaced her with another who was just like
her. Neither hot nor cold, dark nor bright would please her. He
told Seán O'Connor what he thought.

'Oh, she's gone,' said Seán. 'Now, my advice to you is not to
ill-treat her in any way, for they will treat your daughter just as
you treat her. Over near where you live there is a river. Take that
one out and throw her into the river. Then you had better save
her if she fails to swim across. But she will; she will swim.'

Seán Sweeney returned home. He took out the changeling
who was in the bed within and threw her into the river. She
swam and crossed over to the other side. When she did his own
girl immediately swam back to where he was. She was her own
self – as good as ever she had been, but she wouldn't tell her
people anything. Never again did they see the changeling, nor
was their own girl taken from them.

One night I went out with a man. Having served my time, I was
in Cork at the time. I came home and met this man in Kilgarvan.
It was late when we were leaving Kilgarvan, so I went home with
him.

I had never previously been in his house. I thought he was
living alone. We went off to bed. I had been there a half-an-hour
or more but I had not yet gone off to sleep. It wasn't very dark.
Hearing a sound I looked up and saw someone rise up from the

boards and go off out the door. I called this other man and asked him who had been there. He said it was a sister of his. She was quite old, but I wasn't aware of she being in the house at all.

Every night – at midnight – she used to get up and go off out. Off with the pookas she used to go and come back in again in the morning. Her brother told me the whole story, and later I heard it from others. She spent twenty years, before she died, like that – going out every night – whatever it was that she was up to.

One night I was card-playing in a house where there happened to be a travelling man. His name was Con Harrington, but he was known as Con Caobach Harrington. That was an ancestral nickname. His people were natives of Castletownbere.

He was the strongest bit of a man I have ever seen. God bless him, he could dig out a ridge of potatoes at his dead ease and lay the potatoes out one after the other, just as you would count eggs. There was a girl who used to say that she would prefer picking three ridges which had been dug by him to picking one which had been dug by others.

Anyhow, we were card-playing. Others were at the fireside. On one of those the others played some prank. That young man was a bit mentally deficient. Dear me, he took offence, and when the others went to leave he stayed behind at the fireside. 'Well,' said he to them as they were leaving, 'the best man among you has now gone, and why don't you keep him?' At the time they paid no heed to what he said, but there's a proverb which says that a fool's remark is wise but sharp-edged.

So far so good. A few days later there was a fair in Killarney. This boy to whom the fool had referred went there and bought some cattle. As he was driving them off one of them bolted to one side and in to where there was a horse and cart. The boy went in to drive him out, but as he did the horse shied and struck the boy in the stomach with the cart-shaft. That killed him there and then.

Immediately the others recalled what it was that this other boy had said when they were leaving the house. They concluded that it must have been the pookas who were responsible, and that more than likely that he had been going out with them.

One of the Murphy's lived in Gortloughra (about a mile and a half north-east of Gougane Barra). His name was Patrick Murphy. One night himself and Richard Walshe were returning home from Macroom, in a horse and cart. When they reached Ballingeary Patrick was found to be dead in the cart. He had died suddenly, God save us from the like!

In Derrynabourka, adjacent to Gortloughra, there lived a girl of the Learys. After dinner one day her father told her to go and see how the cows were. She set off, east the road and down to Coomdorougha. At that time Patrick had been a while dead. He appeared to her, in broad daylight, and gave her a round-offering, requesting her to pay, on his behalf, a round at Gougane Barra. What amount he gave her I am not sure – a half-crown or something like that. Anyhow, she paid the round, and no one ever afterwards saw him.

That's no lie. It is now over forty years since the event happened. He must have had some worry – having died without the priest, as he did.

About thirty-two years ago I was here. I had a cow and, at this time of the year, I would have to be up early to put her out to graze. I would be up early and Ansty would have the fire lighted up when I returned home.

One morning, anyhow, I got up and set off back the road. A fine summer morning it was. Then, away over from where I was, in Gortafluddig, I heard the din of fighting and of women crying, and the clatter of sticks being struck one off the other. Hearing all that weeping and hubbub frightened me, I assure you. Both men and women seemed to be involved, but I could see no one, and that was what amazed me. To get a better view I went further up the road. Still I could see nothing, but the wailing continued. Then it occurred to me that maybe someone's cows had broken in to a neighbour's garden or field, that they had been seen, and that's what the rumpus was about. I could see nothing, but eventually the wailing moved further away from me – north-east over the hill-top. I came back in home saying to myself that I would hear all about it later on. But I didn't, and so the matter rested.

However, there happened to be in Gortafluddig a woman who said to her daughter one evening: 'I'll go for the cows. The men are busy today.' She went off, but wasn't returning. Her daughter wondered why, so she set off to find out. Outside she found her dead, God save all present!

That was my experience of the good people, for it is they who had been there. It was no living people. They must have swept off the woman that morning.

Whenever wailing or lamentation of the kind I have mentioned was heard something was sure to follow it. Someone would have been sick or dying, or some calamity was about to occur. It would have been a presentiment.

One of the Learys lived in Gortafluddig. He was known as Batt Cáit. He was a farmer. East in Ballingeary there was a shoemaker – Diarmaid Cadogan. He was married, and his wife died. He had two brothers who lived at this side of Bantry and wanted to have word sent to them that his wife was to be buried in Kilmacalogue (near Kealkil, and about mid-way between Keimaneigh and Bantry).

It was Batt Cáit who went back with this information. He and Diarmaid were great friends. He put on his white woollen jacket and headed off back through Keimaneigh, and across the hill from there. That would have been a short-cut. Going through Keimaneigh he decided to called to Seán a' Chéama (Sweeney). He spent a while with him and then headed off again. On the way there was another house, and he was very well acquainted with the man of the house. He was known as Tadhg na Cásca – Tadhg Harrington. With him he spent another while, and then he set out again. By then it was evening. Leading from there was an old boreen, and he decided to take that too as a short-cut. Night fell before he had travelled very far. He continued on, and after a while he crossed a stream.

Not far beyond the stream he saw another house a little bit in from where he was. He thought that must surely be the house he wanted to get to. He went up to the door and opened it, and inside he saw a houseful of people. He looked around him, and there were men, women and children.

'Welcome, Batt,' they all said to him.

'Ah,' said he, 'how come that you all know Batt and that Batt knows none of you?'

'Oh, we know you,' said they.

There they were – young and old, big and small. He told them why he had come and where he was going. Then one of them told him that he wasn't in the right house at all, but they sent a boy to accompany him further west. He went with him as far as the door and left him there.

The people of the house got out of bed, and they were really surprised when they saw him. He told them why he had come. He had never previously been in that house. After a while he told them how a boy had accompanied him from the house nearby. They questioned him and he told them where that house was and how they would recognise it.

'Ah,' said they, 'there's no house there. You are mistaken.'

'I'm not,' said Batt. 'There is a house there, and only that there is they wouldn't have sent a boy with me to show me the way here.'

'Great God Almighty,' said the man of the house, 'I have never heard the likes.'

They waited until daylight, and then they both went east. They went as far as the stream. Batt had that as his mark for the house, but now there was no sign of the house, nor was there any trace of it. It was the good people who had been there, and it is they who had the house. Often a thing like that happened.

In Bantry there was another man, named Denis Flynn. He used to buy fresh fish in Bantry and take it to Macroom to sell. Round about the month of August the boats came in early, filled with mackerel and sprats. Denis purchased a cart-load. 'Now,' said he to himself, 'we have the cool of night. The fish is fresh, and I'll go off to Macroom.'

He got himself ready. He reached Kealkil, and the night was fine and bright. He then came on to Keimaneigh. There he heard a fiddle being played. Having glanced around he saw a fine big house a bit in off the road, but where previously there had never been a house. That astonished him. He stopped his horse and went up to the house. He went in, and there, inside, he saw a big gathering. They greeted him, and apparently they recognised him. If so, he knew none of them, nor could he make out what was afoot.

They were dancing. He spent a quarter of an hour watching them, but he failed to recognise any of them, nor had he previously seen any of them, as far as he could make out. He was about to leave when one of the boys tipped him on the shoulder.

'You haven't given anything to the fiddler,' said he.

'Oh, I beg your pardon,' said Denis; 'It was that I overlooked it. It never occurred to me.' Then he took out a fourpenny piece and handed it to the fiddler. The fiddler thanked him.

Denis then left and went on to Macroom. Having sold the fish he then set out homewards. Passing back through Keimaneigh he was on the look-out for the house. There was no trace of it to be seen. He knew well where it had been. Up from where he was he saw a large flagstone. Up he went, and there lying on the flag was his fourpenny piece. There was nothing else there. He pocketed his fourpenny piece and went off home.

On Connie Healy's land, in Gortafluddig, there is a liss, and there is another on Danny Riordan's land in Dirreenaglass. There is another, too, in Coomroe, near Gougane, where the Hollands lived. That land is now under trees, having been bought.

In each of those lisses there is an underground cavern, but it isn't easy to get into these now. The clay has been constantly falling in. All these lisses are visible one from the other. I have often heard it said that there is no liss from which three others can't be seen, and I believe that to be true.

In Gortafluddig too – on Connie Healy's land – there is a tombstone. I have heard it said that under that a warrior had been buried. It is not now known who he was, but the tombstone has been there for centuries. It is quite a distance from the liss. Looking at it one would come to the conclusion that someone had been buried there. There are stones there. In Rossalougha, over across the Lee from here, there is a piece of land. It is called the Seanchoill (i.e., The Old Wood). There, in olden times, there was a wood, but it was cut down. Up through it there is a short-cut to Dirrenlunnig. Some of that path is still there, and underneath it there is a vault. Litter and furze have now grown over that. There are no tree roots. People believed that there must be something beneath the path, and we often considered going there to search. There must be something there – a vault or chamber of some sort.

There was a man in Rossmore (east of Inchigeela). He had been a constable, but was dismissed. His name was John Cronin. He had come from Gorteenakilla (north of Ballingeary). A brother of his had a farm at the top of Rossmore. On that land there was a liss. John went to live with him after he had been dismissed.

John set out and went about digging up the liss. Around it there was a big wide fence, which he knocked down. His objective was to add to the land. At the time Father Hurley was parish priest of Iveleary. He came to talk to him and he advised him not to meddle with the liss, but he paid no heed to him. He claimed that he was doing no one any harm, and he continued to dig up the liss.

Then, one Saturday, himself and his brother went to Macroom. East of where they lived, in Rossmore, there was a house which he frequently visited. On the way home in the evening he called in there, and his brother carried on west home. He said he wouldn't delay – that he would follow his brother home. He spent a while in the house. Night fell, and then he set out.

His brother was expecting him, but he wasn't turning up. Eventually, it being bed-time, they decided they had better go east. They did, but he wasn't there. They were told that he hadn't delayed more than an hour. They set out to search for him, but they met no one who had seen him. Having got lamps, they went from house to house. They had to give up, having failed to get any tidings of him.

Three weeks later a man happened to be at the foot of Shehy (a mountain lying between Iveleary and Bantry) catching foxcubs to send to some gentry. On the mountain there he came across John Cronin dead, but with no visible scar nor mark. He seemed to have died a natural death.

To get to where he was found he would have had to cross the Lee, on which there had been an enormous flood. It was unbelievable that he could have crossed south from Rossmore on that particular night. He would have had to go east to Toone's Bridge, or come to Inchigeela, and then go off south. It was never found out what had happened to him or what it was that put him astray. He hadn't been drunk. It might have been some hallucination which sent him straying. Anyhow, he shouldn't have knocked down the fence.

It has been said that anyone ripping up a liss would have no luck, and so people were afraid to lay a hand on them.

I think that the Firbolgs, in olden times, lived in the lisses. I have heard it said that they were big, strong men. People had come to the conclusion that it was they who built the lisses, but that they were later evicted from them. I have also heard it said that gold was hidden in them. However, I can't remember hearing of anyone who had ever found any of that.

People never liked to till a liss. They would only allow cattle into them. That was harmless. It was said that they should never be ploughed up. However, I have seen a liss which had ridge traces. That was in Kerry, near Kilgarvan. Potatoes or oats must sometime have been sown there.

9. Charms and Superstitious Practices

Old women engaged in a superstitious practice to dispel disease. To do that they would boil herbs. They then could have the disease sent from one place to another. So that that might happen they would throw over a farm boundary the water in which the herbs had been boiled. I have never seen it being done. It was an evil practice.

For calves suffering from black-quarter they engaged in another practice – to get it sent from you to me. Black-quarter killed the calves.

They would take that quarter of the calf at night and put it in on another's land. That was often done. That, it has been said, would banish the disease, but the one on whose land the diseased quarter had been put would then become affected. Or should calves, or cows, or even hens, contract any other disease it would be banished in the same way. Those people didn't mind where it went once they had got it away from themselves.

Hens often got a disease which was infectious. It would affect every hen which one might have unless it was stopped and some cure found for it. Often a dead hen was thrown across the boundary fence so as to get rid of that disease.

Long ago, too, people used to take butter from each other. It was women mostly who did that – with superstitious acts. They would go out early on a May Day morning to see where the first smoke appeared.

One of those women was out, and she saw the smoke rise from a chimney. 'Your smoke turn towards me,' said she, 'and also your butter, though I don't like asking for it. Come butter, come butter, you tusk-toothed hag!' In that way they would take away a whole year's butter.

They would also be keeping an eye on the three-boundary water – at a spot where the land of two farmers bounded that of a third. That water they would take from the stream early on a May Day morning, and the first to take it would be able to take away from the other two the whole of that year's butter.

I knew a man who, one night, happened to be on his way home from Coolea. Coming from Ballingeary he was, and he had relatives in Coolea. It was a May Day eve. He reached a spot from which he could take a short-cut across the hill. He saw a fire on the hill-top. That surprised him, it being quite late in the night. He went towards it, and what he saw was a woman and her daughter with a spinning wheel – engaged in taking off someone's butter. So that they shouldn't see him he went down on his knees. Then he recognised who they were.

The woman would turn the wheel, just as if she were spinning, and then her daughter would whirl it backwards. He spent a quarter of an hour keeping an eye on the pair and their goings-on. They were saying nothing – only alternately spinning the wheel forwards and backwards, each in turn.

Long ago there were people who would go to the graveyard and remove the hand of a dead person whose body was in a grave. They would take it home and place it under the cream-tub. It was said that they would then have double their normal butter-yield. That, I know, was being done, and it was in the night-time those people went to the graveyard. It was the right hand, I think, they would take with them.

A Ballyvourney woman went out to the graveyard one night to cut off a dead man's hand. The priest caught her in the act; he was going on a sick-call. Hadn't she great courage? Both men and women used to do it.

It was said that the extra height of cream which would set in the cream-tub would be the same as the length of the index finger of the hand taken.

Peaid Buí (Lynch – the poet) had the rat-charm. He was a native of Ballyvourney, but he spent his life around Kilgarvan and Coolea. He had all sorts of charms. The priest didn't like it at all. He could send the rats to you or send them away from you.

With those charms the rats could be sent from one place to another, whatever power it was that the charm-workers had. However, if they were being sent far away they would have to be provided with a lodging for the night, somewhere about half-way. They had to be ordered to stay in such and such a place for the night, and that they would certainly do. There, without fail, they were sure to cause some damage. You know, you would send them only to someone you didn't like or against whom you had some grudge. And, by God, anyone who might have them for a night would certainly discover that it was not for his good.

They were sent to Dermot O'Leary in Gortnacarriga (in Kilgarvan). Whoever it was who sent them had ordered them to eat his boots and, by Jove, so they did. They ate them into tatters. Whatever the rats might be ordered to do they would certainly do it.

10. Ailments, Diseases and Cures

I remember when I lost my leg there was an old woman west beside us in Kilgarvan. Her name was Mary Doyle. She made cures with herbs. When she heard what had happened to me she said it was the pookas who had caused it, but that she could cure me.

She came and got a big tub. She boiled some herbs or other in a pot. She put urine in the pot and then threw in the herbs. She stripped me of my clothes and put me standing into the tub. While she was engaged on the preparation I heard her talking to my mother. I knew that it was my leg they were discussing.

Seeing the tub and the water I feared that they would completely kill me. By God, I sneaked away and hid outside beside a fence, but they followed me. I ran from them, but two or three of them got around me and captured me. I was put back into the tub and, of course, I was crying and screaming. There I was left for a while. I was then taken out, but I wasn't cured. She failed to cure me, and so did the doctors, and that's how I have been ever since.

Should you have *warts* and put your spittle on them in the morning while still fasting that would cure them, provided it was done on successive mornings while fasting. It was often done. Or should you come across a well where you had thought there was no well and wash the warts in it three times, I have heard that that too would do. Often you would see a little well in a rock or in a crevice, but had you been aware of its being there it would then be worthless. Or should there be a little hollow in a rock or in a stone in which water would stay when the weather wasn't over-dry, that water, too, would cure them.

You would often see warts on children. Rarely would many of them be on grown-ups. They are caused, I would say, by some impurity in the blood; that's what the old women used to say. I have often seen a child whose hands were full of them.

There was also another cure: to fill a paper bag with stones – a stone for each wart on the hand – and throw it away on the road where someone would be sure to find it. When someone picked up the bag the child's warts would then disappear and come on the one who had picked up the bag. That, I know, used to be done, but how successful it was I am not sure. It was some sort of a superstition, I suppose.

The cure for *evil* was to go on a dry diet-course for five weeks. That meant taking neither water nor tea nor milk – nothing only dry food. That would cure it. Evil is hereditary. It rarely affects anyone now, but many suffered from it in olden times.

In days gone by many people suffered from *scurvy*. I see it on no one now. It was a rash which came on the face, and an unsightly thing it was. It affected many people, but there was a cure for it. In certain boggy grounds there is a marly yellow subsoil. That would be made into a sort of cake and put on the fire to harden. It would then be crushed into a fine powder and sprinkled over the scurvy. That would cure it.

A person bed-ridden for years would get *bedsore*. If a box were filled with clay and placed under the bed, with a basin of water on top of it, the patient would never get galled. I have seen that being proved. The basin should be refilled with fresh water each morning. I know of nothing else that would keep the patient from becoming galled. I saw a woman who had been bed-ridden for fifteen years, and that kept her from getting galled. If only people realised it, clay has got great curative properties. That was well-known in olden times, but I have never heard of any doctors who availed of it.

A *pustule* is a bad sort. There is in it a worm, but not in a boil. A pustule would leave a permanent mark, but a boil wouldn't. Burdock is the cure for it. It would kill the worm, and no mark would remain.

On blackening there used to be a wrapping-paper.[18] That was used as a cure for *boils* – by placing it on them. It would cause the boil to break. In that paper there would be some sort of oil – from the blackening – and it was that which effected the cure.

Cow-dung, too, was often applied to boils, and a good cure it was. It would draw the boil and get it to break. It used also to be applied to evil at its first appearance. It would be red at the start, and then it would swell up like a boil. For a while you wouldn't be sure whether it was the evil or a boil. The boil would turn black.

Nine times the cow-dung would be put on the boil. There are herbs in cow-dung, and that's what gives it its healing properties. The cow eats all sorts of herbs.

I have seen, too, cures for *burns* and *scalds*. Oatmeal would be boiled and cream mixed with it while it was being cooked. While being boiled the oil which would rise to the top would be removed with a spoon. That would be put into a cup and applied to the burn with a goose-quill. That's the best cure of all for burns and scalds.

I saw a child who had got his hand burned in the fire. His mother got a bottle from the chemist, but that only drove it mad. It was useless. It didn't cure it. I recommended this cure, but they had no regard for it; they would rather go to the chemist. Eventually they tried it, and it proved successful, I assure you.

Lots of people long ago used to get *diarrhoea*. I saw a man who had it and was nearly worn out from it; he was utterly exhausted. Blue-stone had become available at the time, and someone advised this man to get a bit of it and to chew and swallow it. He did as he had been advised and, by heavens, it cured him.

In blue-stone there is a poison. The man must have got some poison in his stomach which was causing the upset and which the blue-stone counteracted. One would need to take only a little bit of it – the size of a hen's eye – and suck it as one would a sweet.

I remember my father, God rest his soul, getting diarrhoea, and he being failing to get any cure for it. He had been working standing in water the year of the Board of Works – after the Famine year. It was mid-winter. He with others had been making drains with the water up to his stomach, and it must have been from that that he caught a chill. The diarrhoea then hit him, and it all but killed him.

There was an old woman who practised cures. From her he got a certain advice, the likes of which, I'll bet, you never heard. She advised him to get a male pig's excrement, to boil it for two hours in a pot, then to strain it through linen, to add a drop of milk to the liquid, and then to drink the mixture. Only that he was on the verge of death he wouldn't have taken her advice. But he did and, by God, it cured him. At the time he had tried up to a hundred cures, but they all had failed.

A purgative would have been good, as the stomach had been upset, but it was rarely that anyone took a purgative in olden times. The food then was good and healthy, and people worked hard. One like that rarely needed purgation. Salts and senna were the only purgatives then available. They were hard to take. They would almost sicken one who wasn't sick at all. The senna would be drawn in a saucepan beside the fire, just like tea. When drawn, salts would be mixed in with it, and it would then be drunk up. That would work both up and down, and leave very little inside one. Until it had worked one would feel really sick.

Many, from time to time, got diarrhoea, and I'll tell you why. An old cow would be slaughtered sometime between November and Christmas. It was not at all the best one which would be killed but the worst – an old and worn out one. The meat would be for Christmas, and bad eating it was. It was difficult to cook as it was tough. Gruel would be made from the soup, as people would have oatmeal. That having been made everyone who called in, even if there were twenty of them, would have to drink two basinfuls of it. That, more than anything else was what caused the diarrhoea, and that often hit people in the middle of the night. Should it persist there is no disease which would weaken one more, as that person couldn't sleep the night nor would he have any appetite. Eventually there would be nothing but water in the stomach.

Nothing would be more sure to cause diarrhoea than the meat of an old cow who had failed to come in calf after being bulled and which would then be slaughtered. That meat is bad. Or a milch cow which had been slaughtered would also cause it. A cow should never be slaughtered until she had gone dry.

A good cure would be a boiled drop of wine. Or a drop of whiskey would be good. People also took brandy.

Long ago barefooted people got terrible *callouses*. The skin of the feet would be very strong. Then when a callous came – first on one foot – it would take a long time to break. It would run beneath the skin, but it would be better that it broke.

Linseed meal would be applied to the callous – to soften it and so get it to break. Having broken it would then improve. At first it would look like a boil, but then it would develop into an abscess, and be very sore.

People also suffered from *stone-bruise*. That would come on the big toe of the foot and be very sore. The remedy for it was to redden a pin in the fire and stand it on top of it. That would kill whatever poison was in it, and it would get better from that on. The pin would need to be driven a little bit into it.

When first appearing on the big toe it would be very itchy. I have never seen it on anyone's hand. It was the cold mainly that caused it, I would say, and it would become very sore. I haven't seen it on anyone for a long time now.

At the time people went around barefooted, but no one goes barefoot now. It must have been the boots that protected people from it. It had the appearance of a hen's eye, and was about the same size. Only to look at it you would know that it was very sore.

For a child having *whooping-cough* the cure was this: meeting a man riding on a grey horse you would ask him what would cure the whooping-cough. Whatever he would suggest you would do.

There was a man who had a child with whooping-cough. He met a stranger on a grey horse. 'Grey horse man,' said he, 'what would cure the whooping-cough?'

'To eat in the morning a black hen's egg,' said he. The child was given the egg, and it cured him.

There was another man who was also looking for the cure. He, too, met another man on a grey horse. He asked him what would cure the whooping-cough. The reply he got was: 'Milk from the tit of a hen poured into a pig's horn and drunk from a bottomless saucepan.' What a strange and impossible cure that was!

There has always been whooping-cough, and always will be, I suppose. It is quite a natural thing. Everyone gets it. A ferret's leavings used to be given to children who had it – whatever milk the ferret would leave undrunk. That would cure them. Or milk from the pap of a grey horse; that was another cure, and so too was milk from the pap of an ass. Or to place the child nine times over the ass' back and under his belly. That was a superstition. I don't know if it cured, but it was done.

Pock-marks were to be seen on people in olden times – before there was vaccination. They are not to be seen on anyone now, as everyone is being vaccinated.

Smallpox is bad. It killed many, and still does in other countries. Anyone who had got it couldn't be dressed. It was a sort of inflammation. It might break out at any time. The clothes would stick to the skin unless flour had been put on them. Some of the skin would become torn off, leaving a hole. Vaccination of children is the only preventative.

Mumps is a disease which affects the cheeks. They would swell up. It could affect anyone, and it is contagious. I have seen it on old people. It is harmless. It would kill no one, and it is painless. It would go away of its own accord, and I haven't heard of any cure for it.

Seeing one with mumps would make you laugh. His cheeks would be so swollen that you would hardly recognise him.

Nausea and *surfeit* are much the same thing. The three worst complaints of all are autumn surfeit, a summer cold and an after-spree thirst. Autumn surfeit was caused by eating too much mushrooms or new potatoes; eating too much of anything would nauseate one.

'May it nauseate you!' one might say. If it did it would make you feel sick. It is bad to eat too much of anything.

A young child – one under a year old – could get *thrush*. Children rarely get it in later life. It would show up white on the tongue, and the jaws would become swollen. It would cause the death of a child unless it was cured. The cure was a simple one: to put the gander under a pannier at night, take him out in the morning and while he was still fasting put his beak into the child's mouth so that his breath would blow in. That if done on three successive mornings would cure the child. And that is true. I have seen it.

I have seen *gout* on people and on cattle. Certain lands are gouty, and there is some like that here in Gougane. It is a boggy sort of land, and it is from that that cattle get gouty. Their bones would swell, and they would become lame. To prevent it bran was given to the cattle in April and in May. That would keep them clear.

There is a gout weed, and that's what gives it to cattle. It is a rough sort of weed and on it a black seed comes.

I am not aware of any cure for the gout which affects the human being, nor have I seen anyone who had it being cured. However, it rarely comes on humans. Poteen used to be rubbed to the bones, but it had no effect. It would kill if it moved towards the heart, but not if it moved downwards.

Many people in former times got *jaundice* and often it killed them. There is a cure for it. There is an herb called black-bean. It grows a half-foot high or thereabouts in summer. On it comes a yellow flower. That should be drawn as would tea, milk and sugar added, and then drunk. There were also some other herb-cures, but jaundice was very hard to get rid of. There was really more than one sort of jaundice.

People also got *epilepsy*. It is a bad disease. People fainted with it. The fainting fits would increase, and it would ultimately kill. I have heard of no cure for it.

I saw a man who used to suffer from it. His condition gradually worsened. He was treated with herbs, but that didn't succeed. He went up the hill one day, looking after sheep. There he got an epileptic fit. He fell flat on his face and got suffocated.

People like that needed great attention, for should they fall they would get immediately smothered. They would need to get air. I don't know if the disease was contagious, but I recall people being afraid they would take it.

I have also seen many who were *short of breath*. That is heredi-tary. It is said that it persists for seven generations. Then it would completely disappear. I don't think there is any cure for it, but anyone suffering from it would need to take things easy and never do very much work.

Shortsightedness is also hereditary. I have seen people who were shortsighted, and so were their families. It is strange how it runs.

Wild Fire could affect one's hand, or breast, or neck. Many used to get it. I haven't seen it on anyone for a long time now.

The cure for it was to write one's name around it with a pen and ink. Then it wouldn't spread any further. You might say that that wouldn't do, but I have seen it being put to the test on a few occasions and it was successful. There is perhaps some antidote in the ink. Should it spread, it would eventually kill, for sooner or later it would get to the heart. However, I don't recall it ever killing anyone.

I don't know that there was any cure for *rheumatism*, nor is there any still, or for any other sort of bone-ache. There are many kinds of bone-ache, and they all are bad.

I have seen saved hay being boiled and tried as a cure for rheumatism. The water would be rubbed to the bones, but it never succeeded. No one whom I have seen having bone-aches ever got any cure for them.

Young people rarely got bone-aches. They would affect the middle-aged and the older people. Rheumatism was caused mostly by cold and wetting, but it was also hereditary, and in that case it would persist for seven generations, just as would shortwindedness. It often killed people, and it still does. Not many, except those who had inherited it, got it in older times.

I have also seen people suffering from cramps. They are some sort of rheumatism, and should they badly affect one, or should they move to the heart, they would kill. I have seen no cure for them.

Windgall is caused by cold and harsh wind. Young people, especially children who didn't wear shoes until they were over twelve years of age, suffered from it. It would come on the hands and on the legs, and it would be very sore. The feet of those who might have it would be put into a pot of hot water, and then cream would be rubbed in. The skin would be as if it had got burned, but the cream would cure it.

Every farmer in former times had a boyherd. A certain farmer had one of these who had got windgall on his hands and feet from the cold. One evening when he came in the woman of the house was feeling sick – in the pangs of childbirth. 'What's the matter with the housewife?' said he to the man.

'She's in the pangs of childbirth,' said he. 'Oh my,' said he, and he in agony, 'had she got windgall she would have something to complain about!'

I have seen people who had *itch*, but I haven't heard of any cure for it. There are many kinds of it, and it is caused mostly by dirt. It affects children, and it is contagious.

Erysipelas is bad. Should one get hurt he might later get it, but it might be a long time before it would develop.

The cure for it was to heat up flour in a pot and apply it to the erysipelas. That would check it. Fire-place ashes were also used as a cure – applied the same way as the flour – or a mixture of hot flour and ashes. It would be dangerous if neglected, as it would spread and ultimatey kill. It would start as a little red spot. It comes mostly from a hurt of some sort.

I had a brother who happened to be on the mountain chasing sheep – rounding them up. To get ahead of them he jumped up on a fence. He fell off and hit his leg against a stone. Dear me, he hurt it. He took no notice, as he wasn't at all badly hurt. Then one misty morning he went up the mountain again. The mountain tufts were wet and he was barefooted. Lord save us, he got erysipelas and couldn't get home. It was three months previously that he had hurt his leg, and now it was the wet that brought on the erysipelas. Had it not been for the hurt it wouldn't have come on at all. The heated flour and the hot ashes were applied to it, and that cured it.

Nothing wet should be let near erysipelas. That would drive it mad. It is a long time now since I have seen it on anyone, and I have never seen it come on anybody except as the result of a hurt.

I knew a man who got a crack of a hurley on the knee. He was a Protestant. As a result of that knock he got erysipelas, but he wouldn't believe at all in the flour. The doctor came and put on a poultice of linseed meal. That only drove it mad. He was sent to Cork and, dear me, wasn't his leg amputated. Had he not bothered with the doctor and used the hot flour and the ashes he would have been cured. But it is hard to impress anything on a Protestant.

Colic is a disease – a severe pain in one's inside. It might persist for up to two years. It killed people in former times. I don't suppose there is now anyone who gets it.

People also got *dropsy*. That was an accumulation of fluid inside. That fluid used to be drawn, but it would fill again. There were people whom it eventually killed. I haven't heard of any cure for it.

There were often people too who suffered from *insomnia*. Rarely did it affect younger people – only the older ones.

I saw a man who couldn't get a wink of sleep at night, and he was worn out. Someone advised him to drink a couple of bottles of heated porter before going to bed. He did, and he got his sleep as a result. Porter is heavy, you know.

If the sleeplessness was bad it would be hard to cure. A change of air would be good, and often people whom it affected went to the seaside. Anyhow, one should never take tea before going to bed. That would keep one awake. A bowl of hot milk would be better. Doctors have failed to get any cure for it.

I have heard of people who would get out of bed at night and go off sleep-walking. That is a peculiar sort of disease, and it is hereditary. Lots of people behaved like that, but I don't hear of anyone who now does. It is bad because it is dangerous.

It would be wrong to startle one while he was sleep-walking as it might upset him in his mind and cause him to become foolish; or should he be somewhere that was unsafe he might get killed there and then. It is said that he would be quite safe while he remained asleep. Should he be found in time it would be better that he was left undisturbed.

I knew a married woman whose husband used to get up at night in his sleep and go out walking. He used to go to the river and swim, but in the day-time he wasn't able to swim at all. It was only at night, and while still asleep, that he could swim. It is said that water would wake up one like that, but the water at night never awakened that man.

His wife didn't know what he was up to. She thought that he might be going off to meet some other woman, as he had never told her where he was going. One night she followed him and saw him go towards the river. Then she thought that he must have seen her as he was on his way out and that she had discovered what he was up to, and that he now intended to drown himself. He went into the water, and then she shouted at him. That woke him up, and he got drowned. Had she not disturbed him he would have been quite safe. It was her shout that caused his death.

Every effort used to be made to keep people like that from going out sleep-walking. I have heard, however, that no matter where the door-key might be hidden from them they would find it. And I have also heard that even without the key they could unlock the door. They would get out somehow, no matter what precautions were taken to keep them in, and then they could make their way even on a night so dark that you couldn't see the pooka's rump. . .

There is no remedy, as far as I know, for sleep-walking. All that could be done was to have someone sleep with the sleep-walker who would sense his going off. Should he be seen in time he could be kept in. Then when awakened he would be trembling all over and have fear in his eyes. It is terribly unnatural. It was young people it mostly affected, but it was better that it should be someone young rather than an adult. A young person would eventually recover.

For *headache* dandelions used to be boiled. A drop of vinegar and a drop of whiskey would be added. Some of the mixture would then be drunk and some put on a handkerchief, and the handkerchief would then be placed on the forehead, and left there all day and all night.

For *earache* salt would be heated in a pot and put into a sock or some woollen cloth. That would be wrapped round the head, tied, and left there.

I have seen a man who suffered from *constipation* and whom the doctor failed to cure. Everything having failed, the doctor called on him one day and asked him if ever he had drunk porter. The sick man said he had, but never very much of it. The doctor advised him to drink it, and he did. Porter is a good cure, provided one didn't drink too much of it. It is very good for the stomach. And if one weren't feeling up to the mark the porter would do him good; it would lift his heart.

A *dropped uvula* could be lifted with a spoon. A grain of salt should be put on a spoon-handle, and that pushed into the mouth and pressed up against the uvula. That would lift it. No notice was taken of that, as it was harmless. Somehow, and as far as I know, it doesn't happen to anyone now, whatever the reason is.

And there was another thing of which I hear no mention now. People formerly suffered from a *dropped ensiform cartilage*. It was to women and girls it occurred. The lowermost part of the breastbone would fall in.

There was a man in Clondrohid who was reputed to be able to lift the fallen cartilage. People suffering from it visited him. His remedy was to get a candle-stub, light it, and put it on the stomach, beneath the breastbone. He would then get a glass – a tumbler – and place it upside down over the candle and press on it; he would keep leaning on it until the skin and the flesh rose up the full height of the glass.

I have known people who got affected like that, and the doctors had no remedy for it. What caused it I don't know, nor do I hear of anyone now suffering from it.

People suffering from *insanity* used to go west to Glounagalt, in Kerry. That often happened. I knew a man from Dromboe (between Drimoleague and Bantry) who was insane. His name was Denis Collins. He slipped away from his family, and they set out in search of him. He got as far as Bantry and then went on west to Bonane. There, there's a place called The Priest's Leap. By God, he continued on from there, keeping to the hills, and on Sunday morning he reached Glounagalt (i.e., The Vale of the Lunatics). He was insane. His two brothers followed him back there and took him home with them, but later he slipped away again from them.

Long ago, too, when dogs went mad some of them would also go to Glounagalt. Others of them would come here to Gougane. That was another haunt of theirs. They would go into the island. I remember a time when two of them came and went in there. Two or three with guns followed them into the island and shot them. Why they used to come there I don't know. Perhaps it was the water which attracted them.

I remember also a girl who was insane. She came there too and went into the chapel. However it was to Glounagalt that the lunatics usually went, howsoever it was that they would know the way. They would make their way despite their never having been previously there.

There was an old saying relating to Glounagalt. To one who had done something strange or nonsensical it would be said: 'You are as bad as the man who went to Glounagalt.' Only those who were mad went to Glounagalt, and it was across the hills they all went. They would avoid all roads, and rarely ever did anyone see them heading there.

Of one who was insane it would be said that he was frantic or that he had lost his reason. One might be foolish and still not insane. Or one might have in him a strain: he would be half-mad. He wouldn't be too bad, but still he wouldn't be in his proper senses. He would be only queer.

The moon-change would cause feeble-minded people to get worse. I have often noticed that. It is true. Many things are affected by the moon. Don't you see the tide? The tide and the moon affect each other. From that you could gather that things are affected by the moon-change.

Rabies is some sort of disease that affected dogs in former times. It would spread from one of them to the other. In their movements they would be utterly foolish. They would hit up against palings and fences in a manner that would give the impression that they were blind. They wouldn't harm anyone who didn't obstruct them, but they would snap at anything which did.

I knew a man – a farmer – who had a dog. One summer his dog got rabies, and he bit two cattle and a horse which the farmer had in the yard. They got poisoned from the dog-bite, and the farmer had to shoot them all.

One of those dogs bit a man, and he got infected. He was sent to some highly reputed doctor in France. That doctor drew some of his blood and gave him new milk to drink, and I have heard that that man survived. The French doctors were the most famous of all in former times; they were highly qualified. 'Even the French doctors my complaint couldn't cure,' says the song.

At any time a dog-bite is dangerous, it is particularly venomous. Should the wound swell up it might poison and kill. Consequently people were very apprehensive of any dog bite and would never feel at ease until the dog which caused it was killed. Their fear was that the dog might have rabies and that they themselves might become affected. I don't know how much foundation for that fear there was. I have never known it to happen to anyone. There is no rabies here any longer, but some similar disease came round some years ago. It affects dogs and causes them to go mad.

11. Some Dog and Pig Lore

A sow, often when the moon was full, would come in heat for the boar.

In Gortafluddig there was a farmer. He was known as Tadhg Gaelach – one of the O'Learys, who were known as the Clann Gaelach. In Droumanallig there was another man whose name was Diarmaid O'Mahony. He too was a farmer.

East of Macroom there was another farmer who had just got some new breed of boar. Diarmaid's sow came in heat in the last quarter of the moon. He took her off east to the new boar. Tadhg Gaelach heard of it. 'That,' he said, 'was a worthless business – going east there to have only four or five bonhams.' No one paid any attention to what he had said.

When the time came for the sow to farrow she had only five bonhams. Tadhg was right. People then questioned him, and he said that the moon was in its last quarter when the sow came in and that as a consequence, that she would have only half the right number of bonhams. Had she come in heat with the full moon then, said he, she would have a good litter.

Tadhg Gaelach could tell from the seven starlets at night when the dogs would have gone to sleep. When they had, one could then go and steal unknown to the dogs. There were others, too, who had that same knowledge. I have seen it being proved.

I knew a man – a smith – who proved it. He had three sons, and lived near a wood. There was a man who looked after the wood – a wood-ranger. His name was Dan McCarthy. Not even a flea would move in the wood unknown to the dog which he had.

The smith could tell from the seven starlets when that dog would have gone to sleep. 'Out you go now,' said he to his sons. Off they went to the wood and stole a tree unknown to the dog and unknown to the warden.

Notwithstanding all the learning and education that people now have, where is the one who could do that?

It is said that the pig would hear the grass growing, and I would well believe it. Be assured of that. There is no other animal in the world better able to hear than the pig.

I had a bonham here one year, and if I moved in the bed between six and seven in the morning that bonham would hear me and, God protect me, while I would be putting on my trousers he would be breaking out the door. He had most extraordinary hearing, and he would never stir until I was getting up. And should a pig be doing any damage you could never get at her unawares; she would have her ear cocked to listen. And it is said that the pig sees the wind.

The pig, too, has both intelligence and memory. Long ago we had a sow at home. Our nearest neighbour bought two of a litter of hers. He took away the two bonhams, which were not as yet very big. He set off down the field with them. By Jove, didn't the sow hear the bonhams, and down after him she went. She jumped in over the fence and followed him. Hearing her coming, he threw away the bonhams and ran. Had he not done so she would have torn him assunder.

So far so good. Again she had bonhams. We had her inside in the side of the kitchen and, damn it, didn't this man who had previously taken her bonhams arrive in one night. No sooner had he spoken than the sow rose up to attack him. He jumped up on the settle and she went to follow him up. We got a stick and drove her out, and had we not done so she would have eaten him. Indeed, it was hard to put her out. He didn't call again for quite a while, I assure you. By God, she had still remembered that man. Wouldn't you say that she had got intelligence? Animals like her are very alert, especially when they have their young.

Behind the house here there was a drain, and there came a wet night. I had, inside here, a sow with her litter of bonhams. The water broke in. When it did she moved her bonhams up beside the fire. She then turned her back to the fire and kept the bonhams outside her. In the morning the hair of her back was all burnt.

Nothing frightens a dog more than fire. Had you got a dog inside there and should a coal hop out from the fire he would immediately clear out. Or should you come across a cross dog, you would need only to throw a lighted match at him to hunt him off. I have seen that proved.

12. Thieves and Robbers

Thieves have got some gift. Everyone has got a craftiness of his own, and so too has the thief. By Jove, if he hadn't he would be sure to get punished when someone caught him.

Lately there has been a lot of thievery, and there was long ago, too – even more so than there is now. But it is not the same. Long ago times were bad. There were then a lot of poor people; there are not half as many now. Many, at the time, were hungry with nothing to get until the poorhouses were set up.

There were none of those until the Famine times. Then, when they were built, many who were poor were reluctant to go into them. They preferred to starve outside rather than go in. Having gone in they couldn't very well come out again as they would have nothing to get outside.

Anyone who had been accustomed to being out and about would have found it very hard to stay in the poorhouse. It was like being locked up in gaol. That, I would say, was why people then stole when famine-stricken.

It would have been no crime for one who was starving, and unable to get food, to break into a house and eat enough. Times have changed; things were so different in the Famine times. In those days nothing could be stolen except from the well-off; no one else had anything. There were always men of substance.

The well-off – landlords and their agents and the like – always had plenty; yes, and the English had got big farms. They didn't have to worry about the potatoes. When they had no potatoes they had other food instead, and money to pay for it. They could get anything they wished and, by Jove, they didn't die.

Those people feared that the poor, when hungry, would break in to them. Nothing would have stopped one who was starving: he would have lost all sense of shame and fear, and his eyes would be alight. He would have been almost driven mad with hunger.

That's how people were at the time. The well-offs would have armed men on the watch lest anyone might come to steal turnips or anything else from them. Many who had no other food often stole turnips, and that's what kept them alive. However, anyone who might be caught could be immediately prosecuted and sent to gaol. It would be in vain for him to plead in court that he had been hungry and that he could get nothing else to eat. The judge would tell him that that was no excuse as he hadn't asked for food. However, had he asked those people for food it isn't that he would have got from them; all one would have got from the well-offs was abuse and, by Jove, they are still the same.

I have heard of people being sent to gaol at that time for having stolen a few turnips, evidence having been given that they had taken them without permission. People then broke into the houses and stole meat and other things. People, up to then, had been honest, and I would say that they would have continued so if only they had enough, or even half enough, which they hadn't.

I have heard it said that no door would be locked until people got hunger-stricken during the Famine. Doors had neither locks nor bolts, nor were they needed. No one would break in. Even the beggars around then were honest and would do no harm. They could be let stay all night, and they wouldn't lay a hand on anything. But, you know, these weren't at all hereditary beggars; they were poor people who had gone bankrupt or who had been evicted from their holdings. They then had to turn to begging. There was no pension for them, and they had to do something to survive. They were really honest people. I knew several beggars whom I would never fear they stealing anything from me.

You would find a thief everywhere. They were always around, and will be forever. There weren't many of them long ago. There were, however, robbers who used to rob people on the roads, but these wouldn't break into the houses. There has been a lot of that for the past twenty years, and getting worse it is.

In my youth someone might come at night and steal a bag of turf. He would have been someone too lazy to cut any turf of his own; he would have found it easier to steal some. Very little else, however, was being then stolen.

Still had one brought home a load of lime then someone might come with a sack at night and take some of it to whitewash the house for Christmas, or for a Station, or for some other event. The loss would have been small; at his best he couldn't take very much. Had he asked for a little of the lime he would have been welcome to it. However, had he done that he would have felt under an obligation to the owner, or he would fear that he was obliged to him, and that would never do. Also, if one had no turnips of his own he might go into a turnip-field at night and take some, or he might take a bag of cabbage. Frequently, that happened and, by Jove, I suppose that it will again.

Thievery is a craft, if one was a good hand at it. Often it is hereditary, just like many other things. I have often seen one who was addicted to stealing, and who spent his life at it, and whose family later did likewise. He must have had them well taught.

There was here a man who used to steal and, by Jove, he had well mastered his trade. He was known as Séamas an Bhata, but that was a nickname. He was as well up as the Gadaí Dubh (i.e., the Black Thief), of whom it was said that no one could catch him. He could steal from you in broad daylight, and do it unknown to you.

South of where we now are there was a farmer who had sheep on the mountain. Séamas an Bhata came and stole a ram from him. He took him off to Dunmanway, on a fair-day, and sold him there along with four others which he had. He had stolen the lot, for he had neither a sheep nor a ram of his own. The farmer heard of Séamas having sold the rams, and he well knew that he had stolen them. Later he met him on the road. 'Did you have a good fair in Dunmanway?' he asked.

'Well, it could have been better,' said Séamas.

'Did you get much for my ram?' said the farmer.

'Damn you,' said Séamas, 'I didn't as he was worthless, and I couldn't have sold him at all only for the four others which I had also stolen. I sold them all together as a lot!'

A man of the Callaghans happened to be east from here one Sunday on the cliff, fowling. East there, at the crossroads, there was a rick of turf. With him on the cliff there was another man and, damn it, didn't they spot Séamas heading eastwards with a sack under his arm. They knew he was on his way to steal something, so they stayed where they were and kept an eye on him. However, he mustn't have seen them; he went to the turf-rick and filled the sack. When he had it nearly filled they ran towards him, and shouted to him. Seeing them coming he put the sack on his back and jumped over the fence. He then headed up the field, at the top of which there was a furze-brake. They followed him, but he evaded them. They knew he had gone into hiding; the furze was quite high. They searched, and spent a full half-hour there searching, but they failed to find either Séamas or the sack; they failed to find him high up or low down, though they knew he was somewhere in the furze. You couldn't outdo Séamas.

There was a beggar-man who used to travel around here – a gullible and simple man. There happened to be in Gougane two or three strangers who had intended going fishing with an otter-board. That being illegal, they feared that Séamas might be around and that he would inform on them. They didn't at all realise the sort he was. Anyhow, they set out, but that wasn't what Séamas was interested in.

When they had gone out on the lake Séamas went into the chapel. There he broke open the donation box and took the money. It was mostly pence and halfpence. Having got the money, he then went and spent what he had got on drink.

The rumour spread that the box had been robbed. Well and good, then. The beggar-man had gone into the island that same day, and Séamas knew that he had. The police were informed. Séamas set off east the road and found the beggar in some house. He had been keeping an eye on him, you know. He took him prisoner. He brought him with him back to Gougane, and there he had him when the police arrived.

Séamas had a halfpenny in which there was a hole, and which he had taken from the box. He put that halfpenny into the beggar's pocket. He himself had already collected some few pence. Séamas said that he had seen him in the island and that he firmly believed that it was he who had stolen the money.

Someone else stated that he had a halfpenny in which there was a hole, and that he had put it in the box a day or two previously. The police having found that halfpenny on the beggar they took him off. He was tried and convicted and sentenced to a couple of months in gaol. Séamas, of course, was responsible for that, although he himself was the culprit.

Down in Keimaneigh there was a farmer. He brought a couple of loads of lime from Castlemore, which he dumped on the road-side. I myself happened to be going to Bantry fair. Below there I was to meet a man who had a horse and cart. I had gone down about midnight, and it wasn't very dark. Coming towards me on the road I saw a man who had a bag on his back. He never saw me until I was quite close to him. Seeing me he got a fright and threw himself into the dyke with the bag over him. I clearly recognised him: it was Séamas with a bag of lime. I never let on that I recognised him.

Later he took that lime back to Gougane. There, there was a woman who needed it to whitewash the wall in preparation for a station. She bought it from Séamas. That's how he used to make money.

There was another man here – a farmer. One year his potatoes grew very large. A couple of bags of these potatoes got stolen from the potato garden. He knew well where they had gone – that it was a neighbour who had taken them.

Then one day, about dinner-time he set out and went to that man's house. He had his pipe in his hand, pretending that he had no match and that he had dropped in to light his pipe. The potatoes were on the fire, with no cover on the pot. He went over to the fire and lighted his pipe, and he and the man of the house were chatting away. 'Damn you,' said he, 'I'll put no fertiliser to the potatoes in future. They grew too big this year!'

West in Gougane there was a man who had drawn home his turf. He ricked it on the roadside, nicely fixed up. Damn it, a group of boys passed by one night on their way home. They took some of the turf and threw a sod here and a sod there until they had gone quite some distance. Then they went off home.

Next morning when the man who owned the turf was on his way to Ballingeary he saw the turf on the road. He said to himself that he had been looted. To find out where the turf was being taken to he stayed up all the following night, but no one came, and he saw nothing. However, he found out later that poteen was being made back in Coomroe, and had it not been for what had happened he would never have come to know about it.

Those who had thrown away the turf on the road were involved in what was going on, and they would have much preferred his being asleep that night. Of course, it was they themselves who were to blame because of what they had done with the turf.

Often a hoax like that, too, might be played on one who was stingy. Boys on the way home at night would go in to his turnip-field, pull some of the turnips and then throw them here and there along the road so as to give the impression that someone had stolen them and had lost some of them on the way. Then the owner would spend a whole week up at night on the look-out but, of course, no one would come to steal. 'Yes, let him have that now!' they would say.

Then if there was one against whom someone had a grudge, the one who had might throw a few turnips in over his gate. That would immediately lead to a quarrel between himself and the farmer. The farmer would accuse him of having taken the turnips, and declare that he was a thief. Then, by Jove, the One so accused would declare that he was no thief and tell his accuser that he would sue him.

Tinkers would steal potatoes or turnips. They would come at night, when everyone was asleep, and dig the potatoes, and take away a sackful. There would be no trace of them in the morning.

A potato-digger would often leave the spade behind him, standing in the ridge or in the drill. Having the spade available like that it would then be easy for the tinker to dig, but if he were offered ten shillings a day to come and dig he would never do it. That's the sort the tinker is.

If, however, there was no spade on which he could lay his hand, he might then go off to the next garden in the hope of finding one there. But, even if he could find no spade, he might dig the potatoes with a stick. He would never mind leaving some of them undug but, in any event, he would take with him a sackful. Tinkers have idle horses and asses, and with these they would cart off the load.

The tinker is very well up, and hard to catch. He would have disappeared by morning, leaving you behind. You couldn't be up to him. At night, too, they often stole hay from the shed or from the rick – saved hay for their horses – and they would be sure to take the best of it. Upon my soul, they knew where to find it.

If you had a good dog around the house at night he wouldn't allow anyone to steal anything. He couldn't, however, keep an eye on the whole farm. A thief could come and steal turnips from the field, or potatoes from the pit in the garden, or dig them out of the ridges or drills.

Often a thief took with him a good junk of bread, or a meat-bone, to throw to the dog. At night any worthwhile dog would start to bark when a stranger entered the farm-yard. The thief would throw to him the meat-bone, and unless he was very good that would keep him quiet. Or if, beforehand, the thief could get to be on friendly terms with the dog and then give him the bone, that too might do. When he came at night the dog would recognise him and expect to get again something from him.

It was also said that the thieves would, at night, know when the dog would be asleep: that they made out from the seven starlets in the sky. That I have often heard, and I have heard it to be true.

You would know from the way the dog barked whether it was a person or an animal he had. He would bark very hard and wicked if a stranger was approaching, and he would do his best to keep him away. If it were an animal – a strange cow or horse or sheep – he would go towards him, barking, and chase him off.

He would also bark very severely and hard should the fox come around to steal the hens. He would, however, be rather afraid of the fox. You would need a good dog to knock a fox, and some dogs wouldn't attack him at all. A collie, for example, couldn't kill a fox; the fox, in fact, would kill the dog if he caught him with his teeth. A terrier would have no fear of the fox; he would be quite strong enough for him.

Rarely would a terrier make friends with anyone. He is vicious, and is the best sort of dog. Should you fear the coming of a thief in the night, you had better have a terrier rather than any other breed of dog.

Robbers used to be on the roads at night – sometimes in the middle of the day – to waylay and rob people carrying money. They all had fire-arms and took the money by force.

In former times, when people went to Cork with the butter, the robbers would be on the roads. Rarely would they interfere with anyone on his way to Cork, but they would be lying in wait when those people were on their way home. These would then have the butter-money, and it was money the robbers wanted. Your money or your life was what they wanted – the one or the other – and if you didn't hand over the money you would get shot.

It was said that the Whiteboys used to rob; that's what the English said. There were also highwaymen, but I don't think that they were at all Whiteboys. The highwaymen robbed.

There was in Cork a highwayman. He was known as the Breiceallach Ó Buachalla. He must have feared being caught, as he had no money; he had it all spent, and he was hungry.

There was also an old woman who sold bread. As she was walking the street the Breiceallach Ó Buachalla was at the street corner.

He smelt the bread as she approached him and, damn it, he couldn't restrain himself any longer. He snatched a loaf from her and ran off. She dropped her basket and ran after him, shouting. People hearing the uproar crowded in. 'Make way for myself and the hag,' said the Breiceallach; 'we are running for a bet from Cork to Croghan!' They had intended stopping him but, damn it, hearing what he had said they made way for the pair.

Out of the city they raced together. The Breiceallach headed for Macroom and the old lady followed him. Near Mallow there was a washerwoman in the river who heard them approaching her. She raised her head. The Breiceallach came and jumped the river, though it was quite wide. 'By God,' said she, 'that was a great jump.'

'Ah, but you didn't see the run up to it I had,' said he. The old lady came, but failed to cross the river; there was no bridge there. The Breiceallach headed off on his own.

The highwaymen had dens in which they stayed. They had a den in Faill an Deamhain (in the parish of Glenflesk in Kerry). That, long go, was a place full of robbers and scoundrels. No one could get to them there as the cliff was too steep and the place too rocky. One not knowing the place would easily get lost there. 'Glenflesk of the scoundrels', was a common saying.

The highwaymen, it was said, had a great collection of gold, and it is said that it still remains behind them in places. They couldn't spend it. Being pursued by the soldiers they had to hide it, lest the soldiers might get at it. Some of them got caught and were hanged. The soldiers claimed that they were Whiteboys.

Back in Mangerton Mountain, in Kerry, there were robbers. Across that mountain people took a short-cut to Killarney fair and back. Two men returning from Killarney fair took that short-cut. They never thought of the robbers until they were far up. One of them was small and the other was quite tall. They got as far as Faill an Chapaill (i.e., The Horse Cliff). There they rested. 'What are we to do if the robbers are further up?' said the smaller of the two.

'That I don't know,' said the tall man.

'Are you any good?' said the small man.

'Indeed, I am not too good at all,' replied the other.

'In my own way I am not too bad,' said the small man.

They moved on, but they hadn't gone very far until they met the robbers. The big man made for one of them. 'Ah,' said the

small man, 'why be jostling with him as you are? Get on top of
him and choke him!' Hearing the small man say that the other
robber thought he surely must be very strong, and he ran off.
They both then tackled the other robber and nearly killed him!

People who went down the country long ago to dig the potatoes
or mow the hay would have on them, when returning, what they
had earned and would, of course, be worried about the robbers.
None of those, at the time, would carry his money in his pocket.
He would put it somewhere else: he might put it into his boot or
in his sock, or he might sew the purse onto the inside of his coat.
That would be a cloth purse with a cord at the top. Still the
robbers sometimes got at them and took their money. Some of
these labourers were rather childish; they were uneducated and
in no way crafty. Still they used to advise each other. They would
also stitch the purse to their shirts. If they weren't well up, I assure you the robbers were, and it was hard to escape them. They
would search them well.

The returning labourers, in the hope of avoiding the robbers,
would sometimes travel back on some road other than that
which they usually haunted. The robber, however, would not
adhere to any one place; he would move from one spot to another
lest he might get caught. People were terrified of them in those
days.

A saying of Tomás Casey's was: 'A thief never left Coomroe or
Coomalougha or Coomhola.' He was a travelling man. He
drowned himself in Poll an Tairbh (i.e., The Bull Pool), in
Knockaunavona. That is a pool in the Roughty River (in the
parish of Kilgarvan).

Anyhow, that's what Tomás used to say – that all the thieves
remained in those places and never moved out. By Jove, that
beggar-man was right; I know those places, and people in them
would steal the devil and all. One of them was a sheep-stealer
who later went to college to become a priest!

I once met a man of the Healys from back there, and I told him
that so-and-so had gone off to college to become a priest. He
paused, reflecting on what I had said. 'I myself,' said he, 'also
heard it said that one was sent to college to become a priest,
hoping that he would bring the others to the faith!'

However, back there there were some who would outdo the
Gadaí Dubh at his best!

13. Down-the-Country Caubogues

In former times a lot of people from here and from Kerry went down to Limerick and Tipperary potato-digging. Their pay was eight or nine shillings a week and three meals of potatoes a day, and it wasn't at all the best potatoes they got, only the chips which had been chopped off by the spade when the ridge was being dug. Then they had to sleep in the barn loft. There they wouldn't sweat when winter came with frost at night, and they having nothing between them and the cold but old rags. Down where they went there was no respect shown to them but they were insultingly called caubogues; they were looked on as being no better than pigs.

Down at Keimaneigh Cross there was a man named Jerry Coakley. He used to go down to Tipperary and to Limerick for the potato-digging at the same time as the Kerry caubogues. They would set out when the potatoes were near being ripe, and wouldn't return until the beginning of November. They would go first as far as Mallow, late in the week. From there they would go on to Limerick and Tipperary.

Jerry Coakley, too, used to go, and I think their pay was ten shillings a week. The food they got, down where they went, was potatoes and cabbage. They got nothing else. They would be given no spoons, so they had to use their fingers.

With them, on one occasion, there happened to be a slut of a girl who one day, when they sat down to eat, stuck her claw into Jerry's cabbage. He immediately stopped and refused to eat another bite. Seeing what had happened, the farmer's daughter got another plate, put cabbage into it and placed it on the table, for Jerry. The slut, however, again stuck her fingers into Jerry's cabbage. He gave her a clout. 'Aroo,' she yelled and she screamed, saying: 'The caubogue from Keimaneigh has killed me!'

The cabbage would be chopped up and salt and sour skimmed milk mixed with it. That was the condiment they would have with the potatoes. It wasn't at all bad; it was better than nothing. It would never do now.

In Limerick it was customary to give that to the caubogues when they came potato-digging. That's what they regularly would have for supper, but they would be given neither a fork nor a spoon; they would have to stick their fingers into the plate and eat away.

There was a man who was known as Con Big Dan. He went potato-digging somewhere down in Limerick. Lots of people went down there at the time. Another man accompanied him. They went digging for a widow. She bought milk at the market when she needed it; she mustn't have had any cow of her own.

One morning she went for milk to the market and the pair were waiting for her to return. It was a long time before she did. The morning was passing, and they were still without their breakfast. Potatoes and milk they would be given in the morning, and for dinner, and again for supper in the evening or at night.

Eventually, when she returned, the pair were inside waiting for her. 'The milk wasn't sound,' said she, 'and I had to wait for the good milk to come in.'

'By jove,' said Con, 'a good thing is worth waiting for.'

He was both hungry and thirsty. She poured out a basin of milk to him. He took a sup, and looked at his companion. 'That milk is good, never fear,' said she.

'It is indeed,' said Con, 'but it would have been better three weeks ago.' He took another sup.

'Improving it is,' said she.

'It was good in its own time,' said Con, 'had it been used when it should.'

'What livelihood have you got at home?' inquired the widow. 'All sorts,' said Con.

'Have you got a cow?' said she.

'Oh God, we have no cow but a collop of goats.'

'Oh,' said she, 'a collop of goats is no livelihood, or how many goats are there in a collop?'

'Oh,' said Con:
Sixty kids a nanny,
Sixty nannies a goat,
Sixty goats a rout,
Sixty routs a herd,
Sixty herds a radarney,
And sixty radarnies a collop.

By jove, she said no more to Con.

That was an old-time way of reckoning. Anyone buying land would inquire how many collops it would carry. That was the first thing: how many collops would the land feed?

A three-year-old cow is also a collop. Three collops then would mean the same as a horse: they would eat the same amount. And two calves from the previous year – that is yearlings – they too would be reckoned to be a collop. And I think six goats would be regarded as a collop.

That mode of reckoning is no longer used. It would be better if it were, for then people would be better able to determine what the land was capable of carrying.

A man named Donal Cam O'Sullivan lived in Kilgarvan. He went down one year and came to terms with a man there – in Knocklong. In the morning the potatoes would be boiled in a pot. Donal got fed-up with the place; he didn't stay on even until Christmas. When he came home he said that the potatoes would be boiled in the pot and that that same pot would be used at night as a chamber-pot. I don't know whether or not he was telling the truth, but he would swear that he was.

When these potato-diggers came home there would be a houseful in that night to hear what they had to relate. They would tell of the fine big farms, of the fine land and of the fine big potatoes.

There was one of those who went down from Kerry. He came to terms with a farmer and went potato-digging for him. One day they made a bet. Should either of them say, 'You are lying' and if the other could prove that he wasn't he then would win the bet.

Things rested so. Having stopped work in the evening they had supper. Right in front of the house there was a big reek of hay. Looking out the farmer said to the Kerryman: 'I'll bet you have no reek as big as that back at home.'

'By God,' said the caubogue, 'we have reeks back in Kerry for which your reek wouldn't make winter soogawns.'

'You lie, you devil!' said the farmer.

'Now, I have won the bet,' said the caubogue.

'How could you have a bigger reek than that?'

'Oh, we have – the MacGillacuddy Reeks,' said the caubogue. He won the bet from the farmer.

There was, long ago, a caubogue who worked for a farmer near Fermoy, digging potatoes. On Saturday evening, when they had closed up the pit, the farmer came along. 'Well, the week is up,' said he, 'and would you mind staying on next week? You will get whatever pay is going.' They said they would.

Among them there was a man who had come from Beara. By God, he had been listening, but not saying a word. The master looked at him. 'Well,' said the master, 'will you stay on?'

'I am not sure whether I will or not,' said he.

'Why?' said the master

'For what has ever wearied me and prematurely turned grey my hair
Has been my travelling from the west each year as November came,
And then only finding myself between the devil and the deep sea.'

That's how the caubogue from Beara replied.

14. The Sweeneys of Knockaunavona

Tadhg Sweeney of Knockaunavona (in the parish of Kilgarvan) was the lessee of Knockaruddig (also in the parish of Kilgarvan) – himself and Brigid Hallissey, a daughter of Liam Hallissey from Ballyvourney. They both had rent coming to them out of that entire townland. That was known as profit rent. It was Warren who first owned Knockaruddig, and then Lowe got it. Lowe was also a landlord. Liam Hallissey was on very friendly terms with the landlords.

Had it not been for Liam Hallissey Dónal Dubh Lynch would never have been hanged. He was hanged for faction-fighting. He was the leader of the Ballyvourney Lynches, and the grandfather of Doctor Lynch who lived in Ballyvourney. Liam Hallissey gave evidence against him in court in Cork. Then, after that, I presume the English would grant any favour they could to Liam, and so he was given the profit rent of Knockaruddig. I am not now quite sure whether it was to himself or to Brigid, his daughter, it was given, but Tadhg Beag (Sweeney) of Knockaunavona had half of it.

The rent of the whole of Knockaruddig was £16 a year. Brigid Hallissey got £8 and Tadhg Beag the other £8.

Two tenants there were in Knockaruddig at that time – Seán Dansel Kelleher and Tuaim Dearg (Diarmaid Twomey). They each had £8 to pay. That land was divided in two later on, when the families grew up. There were then there two Kelleher brothers and each having £4 rent to pay. Tuaim Dearg, too, had two sons who also had £4 rent to pay.

Profit rent of that sort had to continue being paid during the lessee's lifetime, be that long or short. Then when they died it was no longer necessary to pay the rent; the lease would then be broken. The rents had to be paid until both lessees had died.

Up from here, in Dirrenlunnig (north-east of Gougane Barra), Brigid Hallissey lived, married to a man named Sweeney, and Tadhg Sweeney, the other lessee, lived in Knockaunavona. It was an extraordinary thing, which everyone talked about, that those two lived to be very old, but had it not been for the rent they might not have survived to that old age at all. Tadhg was the first to die, and he was well over ninety when he died. Brigid Hallissey lived on after him, and while she lived the rent continued being paid. She, too, lived to be over ninety years of age. Then when they both had died there were no lessees left. The lease was then broken.

Tadhg Beag Sweeney was married to an aunt of Doctor Lynch from Ballyvourney. She was useless; she had never been exactly right-minded. Tadhg, however, had the grass of about thirteen cows – in Knockaunavona – but he got broken out of his land. There was then another Tadhg Beag – another Sweeney – and he took over the land. These two were related. In the other's family there were three brothers – Tadhg Beag, Micil Tade and Dónal Tade. Dónal Tade and Micil Tade had the land, and Tadhg Beag bought the land from the other Tadhg Beag.

Tadhg Beag then got a cottage on the land and the grass of a cow. He also got grazing for a certain number of collops of sheep on the mountain and a bit of land each year for a potato garden. That was the arrangement they came to when Tadhg Beag bought the land. The cow would be on my land this year and on yours the following year, and the third would have her the third year, and so on. It was the same arrangement in regard to the potato patch.

The original holding had been divided between Micil Tade and Dónal Tade. At first they held it in common, as neither of them was married, and that, I presume, was the reason for this arrangement.

Tadhg Beag – the man who sold the land – had three sons and three daughters. A daughter of his married into Gob (in Clydagh in Kerry). She died young. His other two daughters went to America.

Then there was Dónal, the son. He came here to Ballingeary, and worked here and there. He married a Murphy girl – one of the Murphy Rahies. Her father lived in Gortloughra. Her own name was Nóra Murphy. Down from here, at Carrigavrannir (near Keimaneigh) they settled down. They had a large family. There was Tadhg – known as The Mon – and Mike, Dónal, Éamonn, Crohoor, Seán and Pádraig, and the girls – Máire, Siobhán, Cáit and Nóra. Some of them went to America. Four of them – Tadhg, Pádraig, Nóra and Cáit – stayed here. Tadhg remained at home. He married a girl of the Hurleys from Moulakehir, between here and Kealkil (in the parish of Bantry). He died young. His wife is still alive, and she has three sons and a daughter. Pádraig is a schoolmaster. He lives east in Inchanossig; he got himself a house built there. He married a daughter of Seán Twomey of Tooreenduv. They have a family. Then there is Nóra in Ballingeary, who married Jer Shea, the shoemaker. Cáit is married in Teernaspidoegy, near Inchigeela, to one of the Mannings. He is a farmer.

Then, Tadhg Beag had two other sons – Mike Beag and Téid na mBó (i.e., Tade of the Cows). Mike Beag married a Twomey girl – a daughter of Matt Twomey from Derryknock (in the parish of Kilgarvan). He had a family, but they all except one daughter went to America. She is married to Denny Cronin, down at Inchakoosh (in the parish of Kilgarvan). Denny was a shoemaker and a brother of Johnny Mary Leary from Carrignadoura (near Ballingeary). His mother was known as Mary Leary. The father had died young.

Téid na mBó, then, was in the old home in Knockaunavona – in the cottage which his father had got on the land which he had sold. He married a Lucey girl from Foherees (west of Coolea). Micheál na Buile (i.e., Mad Michael) was a paternal brother of hers, and it was a sister of hers who married Humphrey Mary Dinneen (Humphrey Lynch) in Coolea. They had a family, and one of these lives near Ballincollig, married to a sister of Denis Cronin of Dirrenlunnig – a daugher of Paid Rua Cronin.

One daughter Téid na mBó had. She spent a while back near Kenmare. She is still alive. She didn't marry. The rest of the family went to America. All except one son who stayed on in Knockaunavona. His name was Tadhg. He married a daughter of Tadhg Creedon from the Top of Coom (in the parish of Kilgarvan). I think there were four others who went to America. Téid was a cow-herd.

The father of Micil Tade and Dónal Tade and Tadhg Beag was known as Tade Mór. I don't at all remember Tade Mór, but I have often heard tell of him. Dónal Tade is long since dead; it must be fifty years since he died. Micil Tade and Tade Beag lived to be quite old. It must be twenty-five years since they died. They are all long since in their graves.

Then, Tade Beag, Tade Mór's son: he married Nell Murphy, a sister of Liam an Reatha (i.e., of the Race) from Gortloughra (near Ballingeary). They, too, had a family – five daughters. One of these married Aodh an Ghargaire (Hugh Twomey) in the parish of Kilgarvan. Then Cáit: she married Tom Randles in Kilgarvan. And Eleanor: she married Con Lucey in Gorteenowen (in the Ballingeary locality). And the other girl: she married Michael Sweeney in Rahoona (in the parish of Kilnamartyra). It is not long since she died. Siobhán stayed at home in Knockaunavona; she was given the land. She married John Callaghan from Inchigeela. Both herself and her husband have been dead for years, but John's son is now married on the land. He married a daughter of Jeremiah O'Leary from Derrynabourka (in the Ballingeary locality).

Then, Micil Tade: he married Gobnait Lynch from Gortnagross (in the parish of Ballyvourney). She was a sister of Seán Óg (Lynch). They had a family – three sons and five daughters. One of the sons, Mike Mór, is married at home. The other two – Tadhg and Dónal – are dead. Mike Mór married a daughter of Michael Sweeney from Keelfawde (near Kilgarvan). They have got a family – three sons, I think.

Then the girls. The eldest daughter, Mary, never married. She was lame. She is still alive. And Siobhán: she married Seán Jude (Casey), a brother of Matty Jude, from Gortanimill (in the parish of Kilnamartyra). Seán has got a farm near Macroom, in a place known as Kill. Then there is Cáit, who married John Horgan of Coolnagopogue (in the parish of Kilgarvan). He was a son of Diarmaid Éamoinn. Then Gobnait, who married in somewhere north of Macroom. I think it was a man of the Lynches she married.

Then Dónal Tade: he married Sheila Herlihy from Dirrencoirpe (in the parish of Kilnamartyra). That place is now known as Rath. She was a sister of Tomás Herlihy. Dónal Tade had a family. There were two sons – Seán and Tadhg. Neither of them married. And the girls: Máire married Seán Lucey in Coolea. He is known as John the Bull. Both himself and Máire are still alive. They have a family – two sons and a daughter. The daughter is married in Coomlomnaghta (near Coolea). She married one of the Riordans. He had come from Millstreet, I think. They have got land, and so has John the Bull. Both himself and Máire are now quite old – over seventy years of age. Their two sons are not yet married.

Máire Sweeney, then, had another sister – Siobhán. She married one of the Herlihys north in Cappagh. She is still alive. And Cáit: she married Connie Ned (McCarthy) in Derrylahan (near Coolea). She died a few years ago. Then there were Sheila and Nell, two other girls. These two never married. Sheila died years ago, but Nell is still alive. She lives at home. Sheila was a lovely girl. I knew her well.

That is all there is now left of the Sweeneys of Knockauna-vona. I can't recall when it was that they first came to Knockauna-vona or how long they have been there. Anyhow, they were there before I was born, and I don't at all remember Tade Mór. There is now one of them to be found everywhere, scattered here and there, and many of them went to America.

All of them had wonderful Irish and great sayings. I often spent a night listening to some of them talking. All the Knockauna-vona people had an extraordinary gift of speech.

I remember a girl being there who had an illegitimate child. No one knew who the father was. A neighbour strolled in to this house, and one of the people of the house showed him the child. 'Is there anyone whom he resembles?' said he.

'Yerra,' said the visitor, 'shut your mouth and be patient. The wall will yet tell who the mason is!'

Speechwise those around Knockaunavona had no equals.

15. The Twomeys of Gortlehard

In Gortlehard (in the parish of Kilgarvan) there were three Twomey brothers – John Margaret, Matt Margaret and Mickil Margaret. Their mother's name was Margaret Buckley. She, too, was a native of Gortlehard. The father must have died young and that must have been why they were named after their mother. That was common in olden times.

Margaret Buckley was an aunt of the Hyde woman who is married to Séamas Ó Muimhneacháin down below here in Gearnapeaka. It was a sister of John Buckley who was married to Crohoor Mickil Hyde who lived above in Cahir (i.e., Cahirnacaha above Ballingeary), and another sister of his was married to Long John Quill in Bardeensha (in Coolea). They had also another sister who was married to Small Jer (Kelleher) in Derrynasagart (in the parish of Ballyvourney).

It was a sister of John Margaret's who was married, in Prohus (in the parish of Kilnamartyra), to one of the O'Learys. Father Peter (O'Leary) was an uncle of his. Mr O'Leary of Prohus had three sons who became priests. One of these is still alive. He used to teach Irish here long ago. One of his brothers was named Barney. He too was a priest. He is now dead. A brother of John O'Leary of Inchinossig (half-way between Keimaneigh and Ballingeary) married a sister of Barney's in Prohus.

John Margaret has also another sister. She married one of the Hydes in Lyre (in the townland of Coomnacloghy in the parish of Ballyvourney). A daughter of hers was married east in Droumanallig (near Ballingeary). Her name was Peig Hyde. Another daughter married Jer Lyre (Jer Twomey, Coomnacloghy), and another married Mickileen Twomey in Cappaghs (in the parish of Ballyvourney).

This man of the Hydes who lived in Lyre married twice. The Twomey woman didn't live long at all. Then he remarried, but I haven't heard what his second wife's name was. He himself didn't survive long after his second marriage, and his second wife then left the place. Jer Lyre (Twomey) then married in there.

Those Hyde girls had a brother who never married. I knew him well. He was known as Tadhg Mór. He spent a good part of his life in Lyre. He was an only son. The Twomeys are still in Lyre and in Cappaghs.

Those brothers who were in Gortlehard had three farms. I know that it was from Ballyvourney their ancestors first went west. Their families are still there in the west.

John Margaret married Mary Twomey, a sister of Hugh Gargary (i.e., Hugh Twomey from Gargary in the parish of Kilgarvan). John Margaret had a son who went to America, but who is now living in the parish of Kilmurray (east of Macroom). His name was Michael Twomey. Another son, John, is west at home. He married a girl of the Kellehers from Knockaruddig, a sister of Dónal Mór. She died recently.

It was a daughter of John Margaret's who was married to Mike Cross (Mike Lynch) above here in Lyrenageeha (in the Ballingeary district). Another of his daughters was married in Rath (in the parish of Kilnamartyra) to Tadhg Pheig (Twomey). Then another daughter married Dan Kelleher in Comeen (in the parish of Kilgarvan), and there was another who married Paddy Twomey at Incheese Bridge (in the parish of Kilgarvan). A son of John Margaret's went to America. He is dead.

Matt Margaret, I think, had four sons and four daughters. It was one of those who married Pat Sullivan – one of the Bluesians – in the parish of Kilgarvan. Another married Johnny Callaghan – Johnny Pat Nora – in Kilgarvan. Those Callaghans had also come from Ballyvourney. Another daughter of Matt's married Andy Healy – Andy Basin – in the parish of Kenmare. Matt too had another daughter who went to America.

A son of Matt's is now above in Gortmarahafineen (in the parish of Kilgarvan). His name, too, is Matt. He is married to a girl of the Creedons from Inchamore (in the parish of Ballyvourney). She is a sister of Tadhg an Ghruamaigh's wife (one of the Healys). Matt's eldest son was Pat, and he is in Gortlehard. He is married to a daughter of Tadhg na Cásca (Harrington). She came from Kealkil (in the parish of Bantry). Two of Pat's daughters are married in Borlin (in the parish of Bantry) – one to a man of the Cronins and the other to a man of the Flynns in Derryclogher. That, too, is in Borlin.

Then, Mickil Margaret had only one son – Paddy Mickil. He married a girl of the Cronins – an aunt of Denny Cronin from Skrahan (in the parish of Ballyvourney).

In Lissacreasig (in the parish of Kilnamartyra) there was a brother of Hugh Gargary's. He was known as Diarmaid Beag

(Twomey). He has a son – Matty Diarmaid Óg – if he is still alive. He married Paddy Mickil Margaret's daughter.

Kate Healy, who was married to Matt Margaret, came from Barrnastooka (in Kilgarvan), and she was one of the Clann Seamhrach.

There are other Twomeys, too, in Knockaruddig, but they are not related to the Twomeys of Gortlehard, and I think they, too, came from the east – from Ballyvourney.

Tuaim Dearg – Diarmaid Twomey – was in Knockaruddig. He was married to one of the Sweeneys – a sister of Mike Sweeney, the mason. Tuaim Dearg had two daughters. One of them married Dermot Kelleher (Dónal Mór's father) in Knockaruddig, and the other, Peig, married Neddy Morgan (Sweeney) in Gortyrahilly (in the parish of Ballyvourney). She is still alive, but is now very old. She is at least eighty-six years of age, and maybe more. Neddy Morgan is dead for years. They had children. The eldest of these was named Morgan. I knew him well. He had a farm in Dirrees (in the parish of Ballyvourney), which his son has inherited from him. He is married, and I think he has got a family. And they have a grandmother, Peig Neddy, in Gortyrahilly.

Mickil (Tuaim Dearg's son) stayed on in the farm at Knockaruddig, and so did his brother Pat. The land was divided equally between them. Pat married Kit Dansal (Kelleher) from Knockaruddig.

Tuaim Dearg had another son who never married. His name was Matt, and he is dead. They all are now dead except Peig who is in Gortyrahilly, but their families are still in Knockaruddig. They are the only Twomeys now in Knockaruddig.

Then, there are others of the Twomeys of Gargary up above at Lowe's Wood (in the eastern end of the parish of Kilgarvan). They went west to there from Ballyvourney. They went there from Shanacloon (in the parish of Ballyvourney). Matt, I think, was the first to go west. My grandfather then spent a while on their land in Gargary. He later moved up to Knockaruddig.

I think it was a woman of the Beamishes who was married to Matt of Gargary. Where she came from I don't know, but I would say that her people lived somewhere in the west. They had a family.

Hugh – that is Hugh of Gargary – stayed on in the holding. A sister of his was married up above in Milleenatagill (in the parish of Kilgarvan). Another married Tim Scannell in Glenflesk.

Then, another sister married Jer Kelleher in Clonkeen (in the parish of Glenflesk), and another married John Margaret (Twomey) in Gortlehard. Hugh's brother went east to Lissacreasig (in the parish of Kilnamartyra). He married in there a girl who had a farm. He was known as Diarmaid Beag.

Hugh of Gargary married a daughter of Tim Sweeney, Knockaunavona. She died, and then he married a daughter of Donncha Beag Lynch from Coornoohill (in the parish of Kilgarvan). Her name was Joan Horgan, and she was a step-sister of Jer Horgan, who lived above here in Keimcorravoola.

Hugh had three daughters and a son with his second wife. Mike, his son, is married to a daughter of Dónal Cormac (McCarthy) in Coolea, and a daughter of his is married in Clydagh. It was a daughter of Hugh of Gargary who was married to Tim Frank (Creedon) in Coomnacloghy (in the parish of Ballyvourney). She is still alive. Tim himself has been some years dead. There are Twomeys still in Gargary.

There was another of the Twomeys in Coornoohill – Matt Twomey. He, or his people, had come from Ballyvourney. There were none of those – of the Twomeys – who had not come from Ballyvourney. I have never heard who it was that Matt married – probably some woman from the west.

I don't know if Matt was related to the Twomeys of Knockaruddig or to the Twomeys of Gortlehard. I haven't heard that he was.

Matt had a son in Coornoohill – Jerry Matt. Jerry had a brother in Coologues (in the parish of Kilgarvan). He was known as Big Paddy. They had another brother in Letter (in the parish of Kenmare) – John Twomey.

Then, they had step-brothers – Matt Óg and Hugh. Hugh was known as Hugh the Boarman. He was a dairyman in Foherees (in the Coolea district). He kept a boar. I don't know to whom Hugh the Boarman was married, but I do know that a daughter of his married Mikeen Bill (O'Connell) of Cappaghs (in the parish of Ballyvourney). Mikeen was a son of Billy Count. He died some years ago.

Then, Matt Twomey (Hugh's brother) was a dairyman near Kilgarvan. He married one of the Caseys – a daughter of Andy the Dairyman and a sister of Bill Casey who lived in Carriganymid (in the townland of Ballymakeera, Ballyvourney). She was a fine clean-skinned woman. I knew her well.

Then, there was Mary Matt. She was a full sister of Hugh and of Matt Óg. She married Matt Twomey – a dairyman in Kilgarvan. I don't know who his people were, but I would say that he came from the east. Anyhow, old Matt married twice.

Old Matt had an extraordinary gift of speech. He had a blubber lip. He went into a draper's shop in Killarney to buy himself material for a corduroy breeches. He was hard to please. 'Damn you, you blubber-lipped, but you are hard to please,' said the shop-assistant.

'Well,' said Matt, 'on the one who put the blubber lip on me may you never get a squint!'

There was another of the Twomeys in Incheese (in the parish of Kilgarvan). That was Johnny Nóra Aodha's father. His name, I think, was Mickil Twomey. He was closely related to old Matt Twomey who lived in Coornoohill. They were of the one tribe.

Pat Aodha, who lived in Shanacloon (in the parish of Ballyvourney), was a brother of Nóra Aodha. It was from there Nóra went west to Kerry. She was a wonderful talker. I knew her well. Mickil died quite young. Nóra Aodha had grand Irish.

Mickil Twomey was a sort of a poet. One day, when returning from Macroom, he broke a leg. When he felt fit to get up and about he sent for a carpenter, back to Kilgarvan, to make him a crutch. He composed a verse, but I remember only part of it now. Said he:

Get him to come over to me,
    As I am unable to go for it.
I haven't a halfpenny in my pocket,
    Nor would I get a farthing from my wife.

Johnny Nóra Aodha was a son of his, and he was a great poet. I have heard several of his songs, but I haven't got any of them. They were mostly in English. He had a great gift of speech – a thing not to be wondered at, for so had his mother and his father before him. He inherited it, by Jove. Johnny himself is dead, but his family are still on the land. Johnny was married to a daughter of James Kelleher of Mweeng (in the parish of Kilgarvan).

The Kellehers were fine strapping men. There were four brothers – James and Con and Pat and Dan. Their forebears had come from Gortakoosh (near Killarney). Married to Donncha Buckley, the schoolmaster who was in Ballyvourney, was an aunt of James of Mweeng.

Descendants of each of those are still in Mweeng. The four

brothers lived for a while in the one house, after they had married. It was a big house. It had belonged to Bland. He was an Englishman. He had both the house and the land, which he sold. They bought it. There was a flag stairway leading up to the loft. Two of the brothers lived up above and the other two below. They kept cows both above and below. These used to go up the stairs and come down, just as well as any human being would. I think the house must have fallen down later on, or that it was knocked. It is no longer there, or it is not as it formerly was.

16. *Acts and Activities of Others*

I said a while ago that it was a sister of Mike Sweeney, the mason, who was married to Tuaim Dearg in Knockaunavona. Mike was a native of Ballyvourney. His wife was a sister of old Corney (Con) Lehane.

Mike Sweeney had two brothers married in Glenflesk. Their names were John and William. And the strangest thing you could ever have heard: one of them was married to the mother and the other to the daughter! The mother was a widow. They were Murnanes. William Sweeney married the widow, and John Sweeney married her daughter. I knew those people well. Never previously had I seen anything like it, nor, by Jove, have I ever since, however it came to pass.

I remember a man who lived around here. He was known as John Kate Lucey. His father must have died young. His name was John Creedon. He had a sister named Sheila. She lived in Gortlehard. She had married Batt Buckley. Mickil Margaret (Twomey) grabbed their land, although Batt was a brother of Mickil Margaret's mother. Anyhow, they were evicted. Then they went west to Templenoe (near Kenmare). John Kate Lucey also went west, and a son of his is still there. And Batt's son – Denis Buckley – is also there.

It was a Casey woman from Ballingeary who was married to Big Long John (Cronin) in Gortafluddig (in the Ballingeary district). John Kate Lucey's grandmother, I imagine, was a sister of hers. I have heard that there were several of those women and, dear me, I have heard old people say that they had spread the world of relations. They married here and there. One of them married Seán Gaelach O'Leary in Gortafluddig, another one of the Sweeneys in Gorteenowen, and another still Tailor Creed's father in Dirreneanig.

Below here at Keimaneigh Cross there lived a man named Jerry Coakley. Joan Bawn was married to an uncle of his – a brother of his mother's. He was known as Dónal Bawn. They lived for a while in Inchamore (near Keimaneigh). That woman married twice. Her first husband was one of the Sullivans – the father of

Connie Sullivan of Tooreenanean (in the Ballingeary district). Jerry Coakley never married. There are none of his relatives here now.

Jerry worked around here as a labourer. When able to get black oak he would use it to make walking sticks and sell them to the gentry who came to Gougane. He would also act as an attendant to those gentry. They paid him. He must now be twenty years dead.

He was a light-hearted man, and an honest poor man too. He often worked here for me, laying out a potato garden. I would be out with him, just to hear him talk. He had grand Irish, but you never heard English of the sort he had. He used to make up a kind of English that was entirely his own.

He spent a while too as a caubogue – going down the country for the potato-digging. He lived alone in his little house. When at home he would buy himself a pair of bread. One day, while he was out, the rats got at the bread and had it all eaten when he returned. He then made a soogawn, drove a nail into one of the rafters and hung up the soogawn. He tied the soogawn around another loaf which, then, the rats failed to get at. That's how he defeated the rats. Otherwise they would have ravaged him, as in those days poor people had only makeshift houses and found it impossible to keep the rats away.

Jerry occasionally drank a drop. Sometimes he would get drunk, and the police would put him into the black hole in the barracks. However, he was quite harmless. Many like him in those days took a drop of porter, as they got it cheap.

'Bless the mark,' he used to say. That was a common expression of his.

Paddy Thomas (Herlihy), a brother of Thomas Óg who lived in Moornaghbeg (near Coolea), was an outstanding storyteller. I knew him very well as he regularly visited the Sweeneys in Knockaunavona. The Sweeneys were related to him.

Paddy Thomas first lived in Moornaghbeg, where John Thomas Óg (Herlihy) now is. It was Paddy Thomas, I think, who got the land from old Thomas, whatever caused him to part with it. He married a sister of Éamonn Óg (Sweeney), who lived in Moornaghbeg. The poor woman later became mentally unbalanced, and she was put in.[19] They had one daughter. Perhaps it was then that Paddy gave up the land. He gave it to Thomas Óg, his brother. He spent a few years in Cork, working in Wyse's Distillery. Then himself and his daughter went to America. He left her behind him in America, and I think she married over there.

Anyhow, after he returned he used to travel around to his relations. He would spend a while in Rath (in the parish of Kilnamartyra), where Tomás Betty (Herlihy) lived. Their fathers were brothers. We used to night-visit the Sweeneys whenever Paddy Thomas was staying with them. God knows, we all would feel lonely whenever he left Knockaunavona. He regularly spent a fortnight or three weeks there. He was a wonderful talker. He had wonderful Irish, and one would love to listen to him. He had a grand way of expressing himself, and there was no limit to what he knew. He could tell who this one and that one was. There was no one better.

Thomas Betty was a son of Betty of the Dogs (Betty Horgan). She came from Dirreenauling (near Coolea), where her father, Dan Horgan, lived. He owned the whole of Dirreenauling, but he lost it. He must have been evicted in the bad times.

Anyhow, Betty used to travel around with a pack of dogs. That's how she came to be known as Betty of the Dogs. Back in Coolea there was a man whom the dogs always followed. He was known as Mad Michael. He, I believe, was a brother of Big John Lucey, but, you know, he wasn't at all too steady in the head. That was why the dogs would follow him. Dogs, it is said, would always follow that sort of person and be constantly with him. I have never heard it said that Betty was in any way wanting like that, nor do I think she was. It was said that she would set the dogs at the beggars whenever they called to the house.

Dan Horgan, who lived in Dirreenauling, was, I would say, one of the Horgans of Coolnagupogue (in the parish of Kilgarvan). In Coolnagupogue there were two Horgan brothers – Ned and Con. Dan Horgan, I think, was a paternal uncle of theirs. Conty Horgan, who was a dairyman in Coomlomnaghta (in the parish of Ballyvourney), was a son of Con Horgan. Old Con had no land. A son of Conty's – John Horgan – now lives in Ballyvourney, and Betty Horgan, a sister of his, married one of the Mullanes. All the Horgans were sturdy men. Every one of them was as sturdy as the side-wall of a house. And they could be vicious too, by Jove, should they feel that they had a score to settle. The devil himself wouldn't get the better of them.

Ned Horgan, who lived over in Keimcorravoola, was related to these Horgans. He was closely related, too, to Betty of the Dogs, and I am almost certain that he was a brother of hers. Ned married three times, and he had a family with each of the three. With his first wife he had three daughters. It was one of these who was married to Denis Lucey in Coornoohill. Her name was Joan Horgan. One of her sisters married back in Cummer (beyond Keimaneigh), and the other near Bantry. With his third wife Ned had Jer and Con and Nóra. It was Nóra who married Éamonn Óg (Sweeney) in Moornaghbeg. Con went east to Prohus. He married there a woman of the O'Learys. Jer remained in Keimcorravoola and married a Sweeney woman from Kealkil. Éamonn Horgan, the Irish teacher, is a son of Con. I don't know where old Ned Horgan's family with his second wife went, but his third wife was one of the Connors from Ballyvourney. She, I think, was an aunt of Tom Connor of Gortyrahilly. They were the Connors of Dirrentogher (in the parish of Kilnamartyra).

The Sweeneys are now in Keimcorravoola. One of them married in there.

Ned Horgan of Keimcorravoola was a remarkably strong man. He had as a servant a boy named Con Lynch, who was very hard to beat. Ned had cattle out on grass back in Mweengvore (in the parish of Kilgarvan). One Sunday morning he said to Con that they would go and see how the cattle were. They set off, and Ned said they could spend a while fishing in Loughakeenkeen (in the parish of Kilgarvan). On the way Ned said they would go into Kilgarvan. There he had a relative. They met him, and together they went into a public house and drank a bowse. They then went to the relative's house and had their dinner there. From there they set off again, over to the foot of the Keenkeen, but there they decided it was too late to go fishing. Instead they visited John Sweeney, who was known as Seán na Stiallach, and with him they stayed until morning. They were made welcome. Seán went out and killed a kid for the night. They skinned the kid and gutted him. When the meat was cooked they ate some of it. About one o'clock someone of the household said they ought to go to bed. 'We won't,' said Ned; 'we have to go moving hay in the morning, and we have now got the latter end of the night bright.'

Himself and Con then left and set off. They never stopped until they got to Kealkil. There Ned had a relative. It was then full daylight. Himself and Con then spent the day scythe-mowing.

In that neighbourhood there was a remarkably jolly woman whom Ned knew well. When night fell both himself and Con paid her a visit. There, with her, they spent the whole night; Ned wouldn't allow Con to go home. That was their second night without sleep.

The following day they again spent mowing. When night came Ned said they would go home. They came to Ballingeary. 'We'll now go in to the pub and have a drink,' said Ned. So they did, and there they spent the night drinking. Ned never let on a thing.

In the morning they went home to Keimcorravoola. Having attended to some things around the house they then spent that day again mowing, at home. Out in the day Con was getting very drowsy, but Ned kept an eye on him lest he might fall on the scythe. All he wanted was to wear Con down. He had believed there was no one who could tire him out, but Ned had now done it. Before evening came he was staggering, so Ned said they would do no more. Con went straight to bed and spent two full days there. Ned, too, slept enough.

All the Horgans were like that, and not alone Ned. They never seemed to need much sleep. They were hard – very strong and able to put up with every sort of hardship.

Jer Creedon was the same; it seemed to be impossible to wear him out. He lived in Rathgaskeeg (north of Ballingeary). I remember his coming from Bantry on one occasion. He had a horse and cart, having spent the previous night up. The night rained, and Jer got drenched. It was late when he was passing through Ballingeary, on his way home from Bantry. The following morning his was below in Macroom, the first man. And wasn't that extraordinary – he having spent two nights, going to Bantry fair and coming back.

And the O'Learys of Rossmore (east of Inchigeela): they too were the same. I knew one of them who lived here. She was a woman – Joan O'Leary. She could stay up for a whole month if she wished and seem to gain in strength.

In Ballyvourney there was a man who was known as Liam Rahy – the runner. His real name was Liam Murphy. He was a wonderful runner; there was no one who could beat him.

At the time there was a landlord in Kerry – Sir Augustus Warren. He went to England. There he got talking to another landlord – Julius Raynes. Races were very much talked about at the time, and Warren was praising Liam. Raynes wouldn't believe that he was all that good: he said he would get a man on his own property who would beat him. They laid a big bet, and arranged for the race to be run below Cork – in Riverstown, I think.

Warren came home and went immediately to talk to Liam. Liam said he would turn up without fail. The day had been fixed and everything was ready. It was autumn-time. Warren told him to get to Cork a day or two in advance and that he would have arranged lodgings for him and everything else he might need. 'Oh, I'll be there for the race, never fear,' said Liam.

However, he didn't go there a day in advance, and Warren was furious. Liam got up early in the morning. He had a goat, which he milked. He boiled the milk, mixed oatmeal with it, and had a good meal. That's what he always ate; he would never take tea nor anything else of the sort. He then set out walking, and got to Cork. That was a journey of over forty miles.

Warren spotted him when he reached the field. 'Where did you sleep last night?' inquired Warren.

'At home,' said Liam, and that was the truth.

'Then we are already beaten,' said Warren.

'Never mind,' said Liam; 'I'm not feeling at all tired.'

A frieze trousers and a wrapper Liam was wearing. He wore no coat. He had on a pair of strong boots. He threw them off, and also the socks. Then the race started – between Liam and his opponent. Liam was a quarter of a mile ahead at the end of the race.

At that time there were Lynches in Lyrenageeha (above Ballingeary) – four brothers. Later they engaged in cattle-jobbing, and so came to be known as the Lynches of the Roads. There is still one of them in Clondrohid (near Macroom). Another settled in Dromdeega, north of Dunmanway. He was known as Dónal Gíorcach, the Wrangler. They all had that as a nickname. Why I don't know, but they were all reputed to be unbeatable in a fight.

There were Hurleys who lived near Dónal and who cut turf on the mountain. Somehow or other they fell out over the turf. One day the Hurleys went to cut turf, but the Gíorcachs also had a *meitheal* that same day: relations of theirs had come over from Bantry. They quarrelled, and they hit each other with the slanes and with the pikes. They wounded each other but, anyhow, the Gíorcachs defeated the Hurleys.

Had you one or two of these along with you you need never have felt in dread of anyone.

Srón na Béillice (i.e., The Cave Nose) lies on the boundary between Iveleary and Kerry. It is part of the boundary – half- and-half, you might say. The cave is there, and lots of rocks.

There was a man of the Cronins who was an accomplice of the Barrach Mór. This Barrach was a landlord, and a real tyrant he was. He lived in the parish of Inchigeela. Anyway, this man of the Cronins went north to Gornascarty (in the parish of Bally-vourney) to plunder. There there were McCarthys who had not been paying any rent, and Cronin shot two farmers in Gortna-scarty – McCarthys. He then came back to Ballingeary, on the run, and he spent two years hiding in Srón na Béillice. No one could get near him there; the place was too secure. Everyone would be afraid to go there.

Eventually the Barrach thought that things had cooled off. He was, at the time, in residence in Port an Bharraigh, east of Rossmore, in the parish of Inchigeela. At that time, too, he regularly went to Glengarriff to collect rents, travelling on a saddle-horse. Anyhow, he somehow got word sent to Cronin to come to meet him on a certain evening east at Tade Manning's forge in Ballingeary. Cronin went there, and the Barrach took him along pillionwise east to Port an Bharraigh.

The Barrach had living with him a brother who was half-witted. On his way to the stable the Barrach went past the window, outside. The simpleton was inside, and seeing Cronin he said: 'God be with you, Cronin; that's a road you'll never travel again.'

That night the Barrach Mór sent for the peelers. They came and arrested Cronin and he was put on trial at the assize-court, charged with having shot the McCarthys. The Barrach was certain that he would get him off. He was, in fact, on the point of being discharged and the Barrach had nothing to worry about until Seán Clárach, the poet, walked in. He was somehow re-lated to the McCarthys. He stood up in the court, and looking straight at Cronin said: 'Cronin, you shot a wild goose on Gougane cliff and a seagull on Gougane lake, so you are well able to handle a fire-arm, and do you now think that I will now allow you to go free without having revenged the noble blood of the McCarthys?'

There and then Cronin was put forward for retrial, and he was hanged. Were it not for Seán Clárach he would have got off scot-free.

17. *Tales and Anecdotes*

1. MAC AMHLAOIBH'S GIFT OF FORESIGHT

Mac Amhlaoibh lived in Duhallow. He prophesised things
which I think have come to pass. The prophesy relating to the
Ages was his. I have often heard it, but I can't recall it now. In
former times there were farm stewards:

> The steward with his cows on the hill,
>   And his hens picking corn-ears.
> The hare on the lowland
>   Being chased by the throng.

People believed farm-stewards to have a great time – they
having a house and land from the farmer.

Anyhow, Mac Amhlaoibh had a farm-steward who one
morning, when he was bringing in the cows to be milked –
passed by a ring-fort, out of which came a woman who took off
two of the cows in to the fort and milked them.

When he got home he told Mac Amhlaoibh what had happened. His master said nothing. The same thing happened the
following morning. Then that night, as they were at the fireside:
'Now,' said Mac Amhlaoibh to the steward, 'you stay on in bed
in the morning and I'll get up to the cows.' That satisfied the
steward, and nothing more was said.

Mac Amhlaoibh went to herd the cows in the morning, and
at milking time he drove them homewards. Again the woman
came out of the fort and took off in two of them, but if she did
Mac Amhlaoibh followed them in.

There was a neighbour of his who lived over beyond the river
from him and who had an only daughter. She had been taken off
by the pookas. Entering the fort Mac Amhlaoibh spotted a girl
inside, lying on a bed. He asked her why she was there. She told
him she had been taken off by the pookas. He immediately
recognised her as his neighbour's daughter. 'Get up,' he said,
'and 'I'll take you home.'

'Oh,' said she, 'you couldn't do that today. Go to the priest and get holy water, and sprinkle it on yourself and on me. Come here again at the same time tomorrow, and you'll then be able to take me with you.'

He went and did as he had been told. Next morning he went out herding again. Again, as he was on his way home, the old heron approached him and took off two more cows to milk. Mac Amhlaoibh had a hound who followed her. She turned herself into a hare, hoping to escape. She ran towards the fort with the hound at her heels. As she was going in the door of the fort the hound bit her on the haunch. Mac Amhlaoibh, having allowed the cows to travel on homewards, followed her in. There, inside, seated by the fireside and bleeding from where the dog had bitten her, was the old lady.

Mac Amhlaoibh didn't bother further with her, but went straight to where the girl was. She got out of bed, and no one else came near them. She set off with him; he had the holy water, you know. Over the fireplace there was a shelf. 'There,' said she, 'is a book. Take it with you and it might benefit you sometime.' He took it, and he brought the girl home to his own house.

Then he went to her father. She was supposed to have died two months previously. Said he to the man across the way: 'go over, and take with you a horse. Your daughter is beyond with my mother.'

'Ah!' said the neighbour, 'I have never annoyed you in any way, and you know that she was the only one I had. I never thought you would be the first to mock at me.'

Mac Amhlaoibh then realised that he had not acted properly, and so he went off back. He saddled his horse and took the girl home. Her father, seeing her coming, regretted what he had said to Mac Amhlaoibh. He invited him to come again the following night so that they would have dinner together.

He came. They had dinner and they talked. 'Well now,' said the other farmer, 'marry my daughter if you so wish, and you will be given this farm along with her,' – and he had a good-sized farm, I think. Mac Amhlaoibh married her and took her back home with him.

At home he took down the book and set to reading it. In it there was all kinds of information. Then people used to say: 'Mac Amhlaoibh has now got the lot': he had his own farm and the one beyond the river.

From the book he learned that there was a man in England who had a brass nose – a shoemaker – and that he would yet conquer Ireland. That was Cromwell.

Having read that in the book he put his land up for sale – both his own and the other. Three poor farmers who lived not too far away came. They purchased Mac Amhlaoibh's entire property. A day was fixed for them to go to Castleisland to pay the money. Then, the money having been paid, they all went to a public-house. The other three being neither drinking nor spending anything, Mac Amhlaoibh looked over to them and said:

'You who hoard up money and whose fare on the table is
    poor,
A fine fat rent your land will yield to Mac Amhlaoibh
    soon'.

And so it came to pass. Mac Amhlaoibh crossed over to England. Then, as he was passing through a little street, he saw in a house a shoemaker who had a brass nose. He went in and asked him if he would resole for him his boots. 'I will with pleasure,' said the shoemaker. Mac Amhlaoibh threw off the boots, and when they were fixed he didn't inquire: 'What is the charge.' Instead he put his hand in his pocket and handed two sovereigns to the shoemaker. He looked at him and said it was too much. 'Don't mind,' said Mac Amhlaoibh. 'It is quite little enough for you. Keep it. And now, will you make me a pair of boots?'

'Of course,' said the shoemaker. He then took his measure. 'I'll have them made by seven o'clock tomorrow evening,' said the shoemaker.

Mac Amhlaoibh returned and found the boots ready. This time he paid the shoemaker five sovereigns, but he said to Mac Amhlaoibh that he would have got three pairs of boots for what he had now paid him. 'You might do me a favour yet,' said Mac Amhlaoibh.

'I doubt if I'll get the opportunity,' said the shoemaker.

'Well, if you should, will you do it?'

'I will.'

'I have sold my property,' said Mac Amhlaoibh, 'and if ever you find it possible to have it returned to me will you do so?'

'I will,' said the shoemaker.

'Put that in writing,' said Mac Amhlaoibh.

They drew up the agreement, and the shoemaker – Cromwell – signed it. Later, when he came to Ireland, Mac Amhlaoibh showed him what he had signed. He was left with no way out. 'I wouldn't sign that now,' said Cromwell.

That's how Mac Amhlaoibh got the better of him.

2. KILLARNEY ABBEY

Killarney Abbey is at a spot called Sceichín Ó Fadhba. Fadhba must have been a saint of some sort, I imagine.

Having done something wrong, he was ordered to go off and find that place. He was forbidden to have a second meal in any house, nor to sleep a second night in any house, until he had found the place. Having found it, he would then have to build a monastery there.

He set out and kept on travelling until he reached Gortnamucaree (near Killarney). There he went to a house and asked to be given lodgings for the night, which he got.

It was around the month of February. The man of the house had sheep which were due to lamb. Around nightfall his son came in. 'Where, boy, did you leave the sheep which are due to lamb?' said the father.

'I have left them where they will have shelter – below near Sceichín Ó Fadhba.'

The stranger, by Jove, cocked his ear and said: 'Would you show me where that place is?'

'Oh, I will in the morning,' said the boy.

'Is it far from here?'

'It isn't,' said the boy.

Down they went, and the boy pointed out the place to him. 'You go home now,' said he to the boy. He went off home.

'Where did you leave the priest?' inquired the father.

'Oh, when I pointed out Sceichín Ó Fadhba to him he left me, telling me to go off home.'

They went off to bed and, at day-break, the boy got up to go down to see the sheep. There he saw built a grand house. He ran back home and told them all to get up – that no one had ever seen a house such as he had. Down they all went, and what had been built was Killarney Abbey, but not entirely finished. The boy, having got up and gone down there, must have interrupted the work.

It must have been something supernatural. Anyhow, the Abbey has been there ever since, and it has been said that that's how it got built – Muckross Abbey.

3. ASK ONLY FOR WHAT WILL BE GRANTED

There was a poor man who was drawing manure on his back with a pannier. People formerly had to draw the manure like that with a pannier for, by Jove, they had no other means of conveyance.

This man lived south near Dunmanway. He had a wife and a son, but they both had left him. He was old and weak, and he was all day beseeching God to help him. Late in the evening he fell under the pannier, exhausted. He got up and looked at the pannier. 'Well,' said he, 'one should ask only for what would be granted. May God not help the weakness! The poor are to be pitied, for to them no one claims relationship. My wife and my son have deserted me, and my cat has gone from me away over the top of Cummeenlea.'[20]

4. A MOTHERLESS CHILD

There was a man with an only daughter and whose wife had died. After a while he remarried. The stepmother badly treated the little girl: she wouldn't be given half enough to eat.

One night while they were having their supper the little girl sneezed. When she did a voice spoke outside the window:

'God and Mary bless you, poor motherless child.
Your cry is not sweet, nor is your laughter bright,' it said.

It was someone from the other world who had spoken. It must have been the mother.

5. THE GÁRLACH COILEÁNACH

Formerly there were cow-herds in many places. Two of them were somewhere in a hill coomb. One had a son and the other had a daughter. Lord save us, but between them they produced a child, and they not married. Then they were trying to conceal it. They didn't want to kill the child; they hadn't the courage to do that. They placed him in a gap, hoping that the cattle would kill him. However the cattle didn't kill him; they passed in and out but they avoided the child. Then they drove the sheep through the gap, but they didn't kill him either.

The next thing they did was to place the child in a burrow. There, there were badgers, which they hoped would eat him. Instead, one of the badgers took the child into her den, where she had cubs. The child sucked the badger's milk and stayed where he was until he was a few years old.

On the hill there were a lot of sheep. One day a man went up to see how the sheep were. Some were missing, so he went to look for them. He got to where the child was and he, at the time, was just as wild as any badger. He caught him and took him home with him. He brought him to the priest and got him baptised. He then kept him and cared for him.

He kept constantly crying, being wild as he was, and nothing would satisfy him. They didn't know what name to call him, so they nicknamed him the Gárlach Coileánach.

Many tales later came to be related about him for he got to be very glib-tongued when he grew up.

6. JOHNNY BESEATED

Long ago there was a woman – often there was and always will be, but rarely was there one like Mary O'Carroll. She was a woman who never invited anyone who called to her house to sit down. She was so inhospitable that she came to be nicknamed Mary Skinflint. Her hate of people calling to her house and interrupting whatever she might be doing was the talk of the parish, and everyone thought there was no way in which she could be cured of her failing.

In the parish, however, there happened to be a certain man who believed that he could get her to change for the better, and so he decided to visit her and get her to ask him to sit down. Then, one day he rambled in to her early in the morning, and inside he found her busily washing. Seeing the strange man at the door, she flew into a rage and stopped work, to attack this man who was intruding on her.

After a while she spoke, and said: 'Where are you from, you gander?'

He replied: 'I have come from beyond.'

'What's your name?' said she, and he replied: 'Johnny beseated'.

'Johnny beseated!' said Mary in astonishment. 'That I'll do, my good woman,' said Johnny, and there and then he got himself comfortably seated.

Johnny was the first one ever to have sat down in Mary's house, and what fun the people then had over the clever trick he had played.

7. A GIRL FROM SNEEM

Long ago a girl from Sneem was working for a farmer named Lynch in Ballyvourney. Workers, at the time, moved from place to place, and often far from home – to wherever they might get work. They were given very little in those days – only food and clothes.

There was also a servant-boy, and both he and the girl had a hard time. It had been agreed that they would get both food and clothes from the farmer, but they were given no clothes.

After dinner, one day, the servant-boy spoke to the girl:

Dear girl from Sneem whose locks are amber and fair,
No guard from the wind have you got to put round your
    waist,
So get yourself ready and set out for another try
Rather than being breaking your heart for a woman who
    has got but one eye.

The woman of the house was one-eyed.

8. EOGHAN RUA AND THE PRIEST

Eoghan Rua, the poet, was a great man for the women. He used to travel from place to place, and the priests weren't at all pleased with him. A certain girl bore him a child and, on Sunday, the priest spoke about it from the altar. Eoghan was at the Mass. The priest inquired if Eoghan was present, and Eoghan replied that he was. 'You'll have to leave,' said the priest. 'Such a thing has happened, and it is a downright disgrace.'
'Oh,' said Eoghan:

'Because of a woman it was that Louis died.
Because of a woman was fought the battle of Troy,
And because of a woman I am now being expelled,

But it was my folly in love and my lack of lordship
That has now left me friendless in Kilcorney.'

'By the breviary, I won't now expel you,' said the priest.
That happened in Kilcorney.

9. EOGHAN RUA AND THE TWO HERRINGS

Eoghan Rua, on another occasion, was working near Mitch-
elstown. There he was a caubogue, digging potatoes, and there
was a priest's house near-by. Approaching dinner-time a delight-
ful smell came from the presbytery. Eoghan and his master were
together digging, and Eoghan said: 'That's a grand smell. They
have the dinner ready.'
'We'll get nothing from them,' said the master.
'I'll bet you I'll get my dinner from them,' said Eoghan.
They laid the bet, and Eoghan went up to the house. The
housekeeper said the priest was in the parlour. 'Tell him I'd like
to see him,' said Eoghan.
'Go down and ask him what he wants me for,' said the priest.
'Should one find money mislaid,' said Eoghan, 'to whom
should he give it?' She went down again. 'Oh,' said the priest,
'roast a herring for him and give him bread, and I'll go down to
him.'
A herring the priest himself was having, it being a Friday. She
roasted a herring for Eoghan and gave it to him, and also a piece
of bread and a drop of milk. Having got it he started to talk. The
girl went back up and said to the priest that the man down below
was mad – that he was talking to the herring. 'Go down,' said the
priest, 'ask him what it is he wants to know.'
Down she went. 'A brother of mine went to sea about sixty
years ago, and I thought that as the herring had come from there
he might have some account of him,' said Eoghan.
The girl told the priest what Eoghan had said. 'Oh,' said the
priest, 'go back and tell him that a brother of mine went off to
sea, too, eighty years ago, and that I have had no word of him ever
since, and see if he could find out about him.' She told Eoghan
what the priest had said. 'Go up now,' said Eoghan, 'and tell him
that the herring he is eating went further out than mine and that
it is stronger than mine, and that perhaps he would have more
information.' 'Very good,' said the priest, when she told him

what Eoghan had said.

The priest came down when he had finished his dinner. 'Well,' said he, 'how much money did you find, and how long is it since you found it?'

'Oh, by Jove,' said Eoghan, 'I haven't found it yet, but I would like to know to whom I should give it if I did.'

'Clear straight out of my sight,' said the priest.

Eoghan left, and he had won the bet.

10. MURDER WILL OUT

There was a man whom a certain tramp used to visit and stay in his house. This tramp had a nickname; he was known as Ráib. A woman lived near-by – in the same yard. Her husband had died, and she had one son.

The little boy at the time was but four years old, and only the two of them lived in the house. The tramp came, and went as usual to this man's house. That night the woman who lived in the same yard had a cow calving. She calved, and then the woman and her little boy went to the well – to prepare a drink for the cow. She passed by this man's window. Inside there was a light. She looked in. She saw the man and he having killed Ráib. It was said that all tramps had money, and that must have been what the man wanted. The woman said nothing; she moved on.

The man hid Ráib somewhere. No one came looking for him, and no trace of him was found for ages. Maybe the poor man had no relations.

Time passed, and the two fell out – the man who had killed Ráib and the woman who had seen what he did. They kept constantly growling at each other, whatever it was that had caused them to quarrel. Then one day they came face to face and, whatever he said to her, this is what she said to him: 'Maybe you are now thinking of doing to me what you did to Ráib! He said nothing, but went off. What he had heard must have set him thinking.

On the hill the woman had three or four strippers which she went up to milk each morning and evening. The man kept a close watch on her, lest she might inform on him. One foggy evening she went up the hill as usual, and he followed her. If he did, she kept an eye on him, and eventually turned back homewards. She feared he might kill her.

Later she sold out her place. Her son, at the time, had grown up. Herself and her son went off to Castletownbere. At the time the mine there was being worked, and the son went to work in it.

He got hurt while working in the mine. He had to take to the bed, and the priest came to him. He had seen Ráib being killed that night when himself and his mother passed by the window. That he had remembered ever since. He must have told the priest about it in confession. The priest left, but he returned the next day. Again he spoke to the boy who was in bed. This time he questioned the boy about the Ráib incident, and he then told him the whole story. After he had done so the priest went off. Shortly afterwards the man who had killed Ráib was arrested, and he was hanged for what had done.

A priest, you know, could not divulge anything told to him in confession, but should he be told it outside confession he could then disclose it. That's why the priest came back next day, when he was again told the whole story.

It is said that murder will out, often quite simply, and so get the murderer to be hanged. There you have proof of it.

11. HOLE-IN-THE-WALL AND HIS APPRENTICES

In Kilgarvan there was a man who was nicknamed Hole-in-the-Wall. Moriarty was his name. Inside in the corner of the bridge he had a little house, as if it were inside in a hole. He had six apprentices, and he used to travel out collecting yarns. Each evening, when he returned, his apprentices had to welcome him, saying: 'Welcome home, master!'

One evening, when he returned, one of his apprentices, who had nearly fully served his time, refused to welcome him. The master asked him why he hadn't done so, like the others. 'Oh, I beg your pardon,' said the apprentice. 'It was that I forgot to do so, but I assure you I will the next time.'

The weaver went out again the next day. That evening, when he returned, this apprentice raised his head, and this is what he said:

'Welcome back home, my rambler so gay –
Son of the greatest bum in the entire demesne.
From house to house you trek on your little back ass
And your satchels always astride on his back.'

The apprentice you know, had already his time fully served.

Each morning the youngest of the apprentices had to go out and dig the potatoes, wash them, put them down and boil and also take them up and strain them. Then the woman of the house would pick out the best of them, and leave the rest to the apprentices. Theirs would be left in a basket down near the door. Out of that they would have to eat them.

Anyhow, the weaver had a sow and on one occasion, when the basket was beside the doorway, she endeavoured to get in. She succeeded in opening the half-door and there and then started to eat the potatoes. One of the apprentices jumped up and gave her a kick. 'Clear out, you devil!' said he. 'Even if what we get to eat is the same, we are not to have it from the same table!'

18. Oddments

Following the setting up of the Land League land was very much being talked about. At the time the poor tenant was being robbed; the landlord had the power and could do as he pleased. However, when the tenants got together they gained the upper hand and got the rents reduced.

A court was set up and land commissioners came around to arrange settlements and to listen to everyone. They often inspected the land to decide what it was worth.

They came to Inchigeela with a view to arriving at a settlement for those who lived around there. The farmers got together to select some two who would go to talk to the commissioners. The two whom they selected went east to Inchigeela. One of those was Eoghan Conchúr ÓMuimhneacháin, and he went east and attended the hearing. There, too, was the rent gauger, but when he saw those who had come he sneaked off. There was no trace of him when the time came and so Eoghan didn't have to say anything.

When Eoghan came out the others were outside waiting to hear how he had fared. 'What's the news?' they inquired.

'Oh, no news,' said Eoghan, 'only that inside there is a man lathering and another shaving, a man who wants justice and another all out to rob!'

There was a man of the Sweeneys who lived in Knockaunavoña. One day a beggar-man who used to call around visited him. It was the time of the Land League, and himself and the man of the house came to talk about Land Purchase. Sweeney knew nothing about Land Purchase but still he argued about it with the beggar-man. 'Well,' said the beggar-man after a while, 'a single fool would argue more in the wrong than would twenty experts!'

Tadhg na Cuaiche (i.e., Cuckoo Tadhg) had a son whom I knew. Tadhg was one of the Connors from near Mangerton. The son's name was Michael. A son of Michael's, I think, still lives there – in Ballynacarrigy, Kilgarvan. Michael was a bit droll.

Tadhg na Cuaiche was a simple-minded man, and rather

backward. There were no trains at the time. He had a cow, but he had very little winter-feeding for her. Out into April the weather got very bad, so the cow would have to be helped to stand up. 'By Jove,' Tadhg would say, 'she'll hardly ever again hear the cuckoo.' That's how he came to be nicknamed Tadhg na Cuaiche.

He came to have occasion to go to Cork on some business, but he had never previously been there. At the time people filled firkins and got them taken to Cork.[21] From a buyer there one might need to get money, early in March, to buy oat seed or potato seed. A lot of people went to the buyers in Cork for that.

Anyhow, Tadhg set out for Cork. He rose in the latter part of the night, and got as far as Macroom. At the time a four-horse coach went from Macroom to Cork. It was known as the jingle. The jingle had left before Tadhg arrived, and so he set out after it. If he did he went astray, and so he failed to get to Cork.

Having failed, he turned back towards home, as he thought, and walked on downhearted. Not a thing did he know until he found himself getting in to Cork from the north-west! He had reached Cork from the north-west – unawares.

That, ever since, has become proverbial. One taken by surprise might say: 'You have got at me unawares just as Tadhg na Cuaiche got to Cork.'

There was a man who had a large family. Some of them were grown up and others of them were quite young. Tanneries having come in, leather was not as scarce as it had been previously. Anyhow, the eldest son told his father he would have to get himself a pair of boots; winter was approaching. The father agreed, but when the second son heard about it he said that he, too, would have to get himself a pair.

Then there was a big black cat whom no one knew what age he was, he having been so long around. He had the intelligence of a human being. He raised his head and said that he, too, would have to get a pair of boots, just like everyone else in the house.

This surprised them all, but the man of the house said he would have to get the boots. 'Now,' said he to the cat, 'you will have to get into a sack. I must take you to the shoemaker to get your measure taken.' That pleased the cat.

A sack was got and the cat was put into it. The father tied it firmly with a strong cord. He then got a big stick and started to wallop the cat – lifting him off the ground with every stroke.

Being thrashed as he was, the cat used to say: 'Ah, unfairly these shoe measurements are!' He killed the cat.

The Cárthach Mór was a beggar-man who travelled around long ago. He had a great gift of speech. He called in to Betty of the Dogs. 'Cárthach,' said she, 'how long have you been walking?'
　'Every since I stopped crawling,' said he.
　'Where did you sleep last night?' then asked Betty.
　'In a decent house,' said the Cárthach; 'with Mike Twomey of Rath.'
　'Aroo,' said Betty, 'he has got so much prattle that it could be thrown under the wool and then under the rotten yarn when he starts to brag.'

Near Kilgarvan there is a hill called the Bird. There, on a rock, is a picture which resembles an eagle – the two wings spread out, and the head and the legs. It is most extraordinary. It has been always there.
　Then there is a hole which is like a crack in the rock. That is known as the Speckled Door. You would imagine that it was really two half-doors. It is said that when any of the O'Sullivans of Bere dies that it opens and screams three times.

Keimaneigh is full of rocks. A tall rock of these is known as *Carraig na nGíománach* (The Yeomen's Rock). The Whiteboys were the Yeomen. It was they who fought in the Battle of Keimaneigh.[22]

In Cappaboy (between Keimaneigh and Kealkil in the parish of Bantry) there is a hallow called the Mass Hallow. In that there is a hole, and it is said that a priest went into hiding there from the Cromwellian soldiers. It is a half-mile in from the road, but I don't know who owns the land.

It has been said that there would come a war and should one then have a stockingful of oats he would have enough. I can't say if that would have been the present war. I wouldn't be surprised if it were.[23]

I have often heard a prophesy about a war. It was said that the English would lose their entire fleet, all but one, and that that ship would arrive home crippled. I firmly believe that the

present war is the one about which that was said; the indications
are that it is.

It was also said that they would be endeavouring to suppress the
Faith and the Church:

> In the year forty the Church will suffer distress.
> In the following forty the strong will be laid low.
> In the third forty the Church will again regain its rights.[24]

That was part of the prophesy, and it is coming to pass. When the
end of the world comes there will be only one religion.

> Three railings a hound;
> Three steeds a rider;
> Three riders a deer;
> Three deer an eagle;
> Three eagles a yew;
> Three yews a furrow,
> And three furrows from the beginning to the end of the world.

The railing is a wooden paling used as a substitute for a fence. It
would last only about three years. That is said to be its life-span.

The yew is the slowest growing tree of all, to get it to be ready
to cut down. There are not many of them. I have seen a few of
them and I have kept an eye on them, and, by Jove, you would
imagine they would never grow up. There is one above in Gougane, out on the roadside near the tomb. That tree was as tall
thirty years ago as it is today; it is not yet grown up, nor is it even
half-grown. I believe it would take hundreds of years for one of
them to grow up.

It is said that there is a poison in the yew tree which would kill
cattle, should they eat it.

There are traces still left where, long ago, the Danes were. They
knew there was in Ireland a certain kind of stone from which, if
burned, lime could be made. They tried a number of stones, but
failed to get the right one.

Often you might come across a hardened sand-pile in which
would be found their traces – fire-markings on red stones which
had been finely broken up. I have often seen one of these, even
west in Gougane.

The Danes also made ale, but the secret of that they took with them to the grave and never divulged it to anyone.[25] A girl from Denmark called here and I inquired of her if she knew how to make the ale. She said her people did but that she herself didn't.

Anyhow, out on the hills where there is heather there are still fences. It was the Danes who put up these. They shared out the heather and erected the fences as boundaries, the same as on any farm.

Greek honey, Spanish wine and Danish ale: these were the finest of all drinks. And there was a proverb about the ale. Should someone be so seriously ill that it was thought he would not survive, and should another call to see how he was then another might inquire how he had found him. 'By Jove,' he might reply, 'he won't live even if he gets ale.' People believed there was no better drink than ale.

Back in Kerry there was a man who used to claim that the cat was the worst of all servants for, as likely as not, on a fine Autumn day he would be found to be inside in the bed. By Jove, he was right, for it is there he would be!

A vagabond's advice is the best of all. From him one might get excellent advice.

Trying to advise a headstrong woman or striking cold iron with a hair-rib are equally futile.

Never buy a horse which hasn't got a coat somewhat like fox-fur. That was the advice given long ago by an old man to his son.

Take life easy and life will be easy for you. One should always take life easy.

Reflect once and twenty and then you will get to know all about everything. One should always look ahead. The one who looks well ahead becomes very shrewd.

Stealing from a thief is ne'er a sin. Though that is a proverb it would be no defence in court.

'He is worse than Písín, and Písín was worse than the devil.' That would be said of an evil-doer. Who Písín was I don't know.

A house on a height, a white horse and a woman with a bonnet: three things which are bad. A woman wearing a bonnet would be regarded as being well-dressed but lazy; she would be deemed to be useless other than for showing off on Sunday, in public.

A horsebud is a large fly with two pairs of wings. It is shaped like an aeroplane, and it is said that it is from it the aeroplane was designed. I see them around here, and there has been one of them here for the past six years. Its size is what has surprised me; I have never seen anything like it. It comes every year, and it is here now.[26]

Notes

1.–The Mercier Press, Dublin and Cork, 1978.

2.–A dairyman was the lessee for a period of one year or less, but renewable, of a farm stocked with milch cows and for which he paid a certain rental per cow. A man so engaged was said to be dairying.

3.–Introduction to the 1964 edition of *The Tailor and Ansty*: Cross (Eric).

4.–This must have been a mocking dig at Seán Ó Crónín and the ediphone with which he recorded what was being related rather than remembering it as would the Tailor himself and all the older storytellers.

5.–The first Ballingeary National School was opened in 1833.

6.–Keimaneigh National School was built in 1871. Its first teacher was Denis O'Mahony, and his salary was £14 a year.

7.–Denis O'Sullivan's father's name was really James, but Denis had a brother named Owen who taught for a while in Keimaneigh as a monitor.

8.–It was from Master O'Regan, right enough, the Mícheál Ó Suibhne learned to write and read Irish, but it was not from him that Séamus Ó Muimhneacháin, my own father, acquired these skills but from Con Cotter, a great collector of Irish songs and tales and who succeeded Master O'Regan in the National School. Regularly, at night-time, my father sat in with him in the apartment in which he lived. He was a bachelor.

9.–Clydagh is the name of the valley in east Kerry which lies between the Derrynasaggart Mountain and the Paps and through which runs the Clydagh River, a tributary of the Flesk. There, on 8 August 1831, occurred an unexpected thunder cloud-burst which caused a flood so fierce-flowing that it devastated the entire valley and swept off to their deaths three men, four women and four children.

10.–Of this, in the Irish-speaking areas, there were several variants. The version of it which I got from my father might be translated:

> A the big mouth.
> B the potato.
> C the horseshoe.
> D the shoe-heel.
> E(e) the blind eyelet.
> F the flap.
> G(g) the spectacles.
> H the chair-back.
> I the little baton.
> J the hurley.
> K the key.
> L the scythe.
> M of the butter and
> N eating it.
> O the ring.
> P the hammer.
> Q of the tail.
> R(r) the top-boot.

S the little worm.
T the crutch.
U the pannier-bow.
V the little frieze trews.
W the goose-foot.
X the cross.
Y the little fork.
Z the shoe-last.

11.–However, there now, and right back into Coomroe, is an extensive forest, the property of the Irish Forestry Department, who acquired the lands.

12.–On the uppermost flagstone there are two little grooves traditionally said to be the imprints of St Finbarr's knees.

13.–Father Hurley was parish priest of Iveleary 1888-1908.

14-16.–All in the vicinity of Dunmanway, Co. Cork.

17.–St Fiachna's Cemetery is in Bonane, south-west of Kenmare, Co. Kerry.

18.–Blackening was a substance which in olden times, when mixed with water, was used to polish shoes.

19.–To the Mental Hospital in Cork.

20.–Cummeenlea lies east of Dunmanway, Co. Cork.

21.–The firkins mentioned here were the wooden casks in which butter was taken to the market.

22.–Here the narrator seems to have been mistaken or misinformed. The Yeomen were a corps of Protestant tenants and townsmen recruited to assist the British crown forces when called upon and to keep the British authorities informed of any suspected anti-British subversive activities, whereas the Whiteboys were an organisation of Catholic farmers and their sons pledged to resist the exaction of tithes from Catholics for the support of the Protestant clergy. We should also mention that the Irish term *gíománach*, meaning 'a yeoman', might also signify 'a coachman' or even 'a strong, stalwart and daring young man.'

In 1822, on the night before the Battle of Keimaneigh, Whiteboys from the Keimaneigh-Ballingeary district raided the houses of British sympathisers in Bantry and its environs and seized arms. They were pursued by the local Yeomen and military who, when they reached Keimaneigh, were ambushed. They took cover behind a massive rock, and there they laid low until the Whiteboys, thinking they had retreated, came into the open, and two of them, Humphrey Lynch and Barry O'Leary, were shot dead. The Whiteboys then redeployed, and in the course of further engagements one of the British soldiers – a John Smith of the Rifle Brigade – in a hand-to-hand encounter with James Walshe was also killed. Ever since the rock behind which the Yeomen had hidden is known as *Carraig na nGíománach* (The Yeomen's Rock).

23.–On 16 August 1942 the Tailor related this.

24.–Of this 'prophesy', ascribed to Mac Amhlaoibh of Duhallow, there have come to be many variants, and the most common of these might be translated.

In the year forty furze will have neither seed nor flower.
The following year of hunger thousands will die.
In the third year the Church will unrelentingly be persecuted,
But in the second forty the Church will regain its rights.

25.–According to tradition, there came a time when all but two of the Danes in Ireland – a father and his son – had been exterminated. They knew how to make the ale, and the Irish knew they had that knowledge. In the hope of gaining the secret they were told their lives would be spared if they disclosed the knowledge. 'Kill my son,' said the old man, 'and I will then tell.'

The son was killed. 'Kill me now too,' said the father, 'for I will never give you the secret,' and so the Irish did in desperation. It was that the father had feared that the son would squeal should he be the last to survive.

A very fine collection of Danish ale-lore which Séamus Ó Duilearga procured with the aid of folklore collectors in Cork, Kerry, Clare, Galway, Waterford and Donegal in 1934 has been published in The Journal of the Folklore of Ireland Society, *Béaloideas* V, 28-51.

26.–It would seem that the insect referred to here was that which is better known as the dragon-fly.

Another Interesting Title

The Tailor and Ansty
Eric Cross

' 'Tis a funny state of affairs when you think of it.'
It is the Tailor himself speaking. 'The book is
nothing but the fun and the talk and the laughter
which has gone on for years around this
fireside...'

The *Tailor and Ansty* was banned soon after its
first publication in 1942 and was the subject of such
bitter controversy that it may well have influenced the
later relaxation of the censorship law. Certainly it has
become a modern Irish classic, promising to make
immortals of the Tailor and his irrepressible foil, his
wife, Ansty, and securing a niche in Irish letters for
their Boswell, Eric Cross.

The Tailor never travelled further than
Scotland and yet the width of the world can hardly
contain his wealth of humour and fantasy. Marriages,
inquests, matchmaking, wakes – everthing is here. Let
the Tailor round it off with a verse of a ballad:

> Now all you young maidens,
> Don't listen to me
> For I will incite you to immoralitee,
> Or unnatural vice or in a similar way
> Corrupt or deprave you or lead you astray.